Biogeography

Rona Mottershead

GEOGRAPHY
APPLIED

General
Editor
JOHN
HANCOCK

BASIL BLACKWELL . PUBLISHER

Published in Great Britain by Basil Blackwell
Publisher

© Rona Mottershead 1979

ISBN 0 631 93510 X

TO MY BROTHER

Contents

1. Wild lands, tamed lands, spoiled lands	4
Habitat change	4
Why have habitats changed?	8
Habitat unity	10
A closer look at ecosystems	11
2. Clothing the earth: colonization and plant succession	14
Surtsey	14
Krakatoa	16
Plant succession in different environments: examples from Britain	18
Lithosere, psammosere, halosere and hydrosere	24
3. Patterns of plant growth and their causes	25
A desert in Britain	25
The Keen of Hamar, Shetland: a field study	26
Deserts of the Arctic	27
4. Woodlands	28
Practical studies	29
Newgate Wood, Yorkshire: a field study	32
5. The soil	37
Dynamics of the soil ecosystem	38
Unravel the causes: an exercise in soil detection	44
6. Substantially changed environments	47
Lockton Low Moor	47
Competing claims and limited land: land use on the North Yorkshire Moors	51
7. Spoiled soils	54
Farming in Lincolnshire	54
The Lower Swansea Valley	54
Mid-Wales sheep "burrows"	54
Spreading deserts	55
Reclaiming deserts	55
8. World patterns	57
Net primary productivity: the creation of living matter	57
Biomass: the earth's resource	60
Land-use planning on a world scale	62
Booklist	63
Answers to exercises	63
Index	64

Acknowledgements

We are grateful to the following for their help in providing photographs:

Aerofilms for 1k and l
Barry Barnacal for 2., 2m and 2n
Pierre Boulat for 1j and 1n
Cambridge University Collection (copyright reserved) for 2ab
Camera Press for 1a, 1b, 1f, 1m
J. Allen Cash for 1c
Curtis Horn Ltd, Oxford for 1g (inset)
Harry Foster for 2h and 2j
Fox Photos for 2d
Sturla Fridriksson for 2b
Valerie McFarland for 2p
Merseyside County Museums for 2u and 2v
E. Mottershead for 2a and 2aa
Rona Mottershead for 1e, 3b, 5b, 6b, 6g
National Film Board of Canada for 1g
Nature Conservancy Council for 2t
Picturepoint for 1h
Talbot Taylor for 1a (warrior)
John Topham Picture Library for 1d
Syndication International for 1f (inset)

We are also grateful to the following who have provided us with material:

Butterworths, London for the extracts from *Surtsey: Evolution of life on a Volcanic Island*, Sturla Fridriksson, 1975
The Dalesman Publishing Company for the crossings table from *Lyke Wake Walk*, Bill Cowley, 1976
The Forestry Commission and G. B. Grant and Sons (Farmers), Louth for the extracts from letters to the author
The *Guardian* for figs 6t and 7c

Conversion figures

1 tonne/hectare $= 100 \text{ g/m}^2$
1 hectare $= 10\,000$ square metres
1 tonne $= 1\,000$ kilograms
1 metric tonne $= 1.1023$ English short tons
square kilometres $\times 0.3861 =$ square miles
$\text{g/m}^2 \times 8.29 = \text{lbs/acre}$

Approximate conversions

1 metre $= 39$ inches
1 km $= \frac{5}{8}$ mile
1 litre $= 1\frac{3}{4}$ pints
28 grammes $= 1$ oz
1 kilogram $= 2\frac{1}{4}$ lbs
1 hectare $= 2\frac{1}{2}$ acres
5 square metres $= 6$ square yards

Booklist

1. Conolly, A. P. and McLean, B. J., "Brave survivors of the Ice Age", *Geographical Magazine*, January 1975, pp. 243–250.
2. Morgan, R. P. C., "Survey of soil erosion", *Geographical Magazine*, March 1975, pp. 360–363.
3. Newbould, P. J., "Production ecology and the International Biological Programme", *Geography*, vol. 50, 1965, pp. 242–251.
4. Pears, N. V., "Trees in Trust", *Geographical Magazine*, March 1975, pp. 372–377.
5. Pullen, R. A., "Burning impact on African Savannas", *Geographical Magazine*, April 1975, pp. 432–438.
6. Richards, B. N., *Introduction to the soil ecosystem*, Longmans, 1974. (An advanced book.)
7. Rodgers, H. B., Patmore, J. A., Gittins, J. W. and Tanner, M. F., "Recreation and Resources", *Geographical Journal*, vol. 139, 1973.
8. Simmons, I. G., "Ecology and Land Use", Institute of British Geographers, Transaction no. 36, June 1966, pp. 59–72.
9. Stoddart, D. R., "Geography and the ecological approach", *Geography*, vol. 50, 1965, pp. 242–251.
10. Stoddart, D. R., "Catastrophic human interference with coral atoll ecosystems", *Geography*, vol. 53, 1968, pp. 25–39.
11. Tansley, A. G., *Britain's Green Mantle*, Allen and Unwin, 1949, Chapters 1–4.
12. Tivy, J., "Britain's one-third of waste land", *Geographical Magazine*, February 1975, pp. 314–319.
13. Tivy, J., "Biogeography", in *The Forest Resource*, Oliver and Boyd, 1971, pp. 281–290.

1 Wild lands, tamed lands, spoiled lands

'Mighty mountains mystical[1]'; 'endless sands yielding nothing but small, stunted shrubs[2]'; 'Uniform green mass of forest. . . . Towards evening life revives again, and the ringing uproar is resumed from bush and tree[3]'; high plains dusted with yellowed grass and thirsty trees grazed by long-necked spotted giants; icy, white wastes: such is the variety of the earth's natural environments. Each one is the result of a unique combination of rock, water, air, plants and animals in particular climatic conditions. At one time man lived as other animals, before he developed tools to tame the earth. Then only about ten million human beings could gain a living from the earth. Today man is trying to control his environment, to change it so that he can live in larger numbers in greater comfort than his ancestors. Consequently no part of the earth's surface is completely natural.

[1] F. V. Branford, *Ben Mor: an armistice poem, The London Mercury, vol. XXVI, 1932*
[2] F. W. Kinglake, *Eothen*, Methuen, 1921
[3] H. W. Bates, *The Naturalist on the River Amazon*, Everyman's Library, Dent, 1969

exercises

Habitat change

Figs 1.a–m show a variety of habitats which have suffered different degrees of alteration by man. Examine each photograph in turn and answer the following questions ready for class discussion.

1.1 What changes have resulted from man's activities?

1.2 How much of the area shown on figs 1.a–m has been changed by man?

1.3 Classify the landscapes into three categories according to the degree of change.
(i) slightly changed;
(ii) substantially changed;
(iii) totally changed.

1.4 Why have these changes been made?

1.5 Were they made recently or a long time ago?

1.6 Mark on a world map the location of the twelve places shown in the photographs. Outline and name the countries, use appropriate shading for areas of vegetation and mark the location of particular spots by means of labelled arrows.

Fig 1.a African savanna

Fig 1.b Chinese
ricefields

Fig 1.e Arctic tundra

Fig 1.d China clay
mine, Cornwall

Fig 1.c The
Himalayas

Fig 1.f Amazon rainforest

Fig 1.g Canadian prairie

Fig 1.h The
industrial Ruhr

Fig 1.j The Sahara

Fig 1.l The North Yorkshire Moors

Fig 1.k Forestry Commission

Why have habitats changed?

Your answer to exercise 1.4 might have been, 'so man can make better use of his environment'. Let us look at the how and why of change in a little more detail.

exercises

Technology

1.7 Compare the tools man uses in figs 1.f and 1.g.

1.8 How do the tools differ in materials, use, size and power?

1.9 If the Amazon Indian had the Canadian farmer's technological knowledge and sophisticated machinery, what kind of habitat might he create?

1.10 Why hasn't he created such an environment?

1.11 If he had the money to buy a combine harvester for his own use, what other changes would he have to make before he could use it?

Pressure of population

Rank figs 1a–m in order of density of population and answer the following questions. Then compare your results with the classification that you made in exercise 1.3. Comment on your findings.

1.12 In which areas shown in the photographs is:
(i) the terrain so inhospitable that man has not yet developed the technology to overcome it?
(ii) man supported entirely by his surrounding environment?
(iii) man dependent on other parts of the earth for his life support?
(iv) man able to support people in other parts of the world?

1.13 What would happen to the population in fig 1.h if all food supplies from outside were cut off? How would the habitat change if this area had to be completely self-supporting?

Climate

Look at fig 1n. This cave painting was made by a man living in the middle of the Sahara desert sometime between 4–2000 BC

1.14 What activities are the men engaged in?

1.15 Do they live like this here today?

1.16 What do the boats and cattle tell you about the climate?

1.17 Try to find other examples, and write an essay on the effect, of climatic change through time on one of the earth's habitats.

Fig 1.m Peruvian terraces

Culture

As you can see from fig 1.m, the Peruvian Indians substantially altered their habitat as long ago as AD 200 to 600. Their achievements were remarkable considering their very tough environment and their lack of draught animals and wheeled vehicles. What power do you think they used?

They put every hectare of land to work, either by terracing steep slopes or by irrigating valley bottoms with vast and intricate networks of channels. They also produced wonderful pottery, textiles, and ornaments of gold and silver. They erected great stone temples to honour their animal-like gods and furnished tombs worthy of their revered ancestors. They had a governing elite, whose main preoccupations were religion and war, beneath which there was a complicated social hierarchy of peasants, engineers and gorgeously-attired warriors. The community and church lands were worked in common by the people under the direction of a local chief; and communal labour was requisitioned for the upkeep of the irrigation system, the terraces, the roads and other public works. Thus Peruvian religion, social organization and agriculture were all bound up together. So great was their cultural influence on the environment that signs of it are still visible today.

The Inca empire took over after this classic period in Peruvian history. It flourished and expanded but finally toppled at the hands of the sixteenth-century Spanish adventurers. The flowering of such a civilization is attributed mainly to the efforts of man—to his initiative and his inventiveness, to his ability to organize and use the human and territorial resources at his disposal. By the nineteenth century the Peruvian Indians' empire had disintegrated and the people had reverted to peasantry, scratching a living from the earth. Why there should be this rise and fall in man's fortunes is a much debated problem to which no one knows the complete answer. 'The progress of the human race is best compared to a gigantic pendulum which forever swings forward and backward.[1]'

[1]H. W. van Loon, *The Story of Mankind,* Harrap, 1948

Fig 1.n

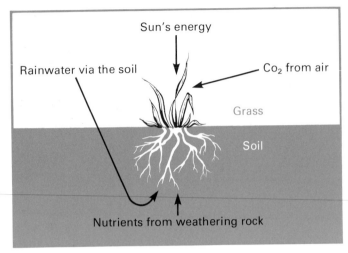

Fig 1.p

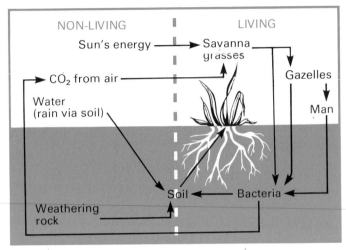

Fig 1.r

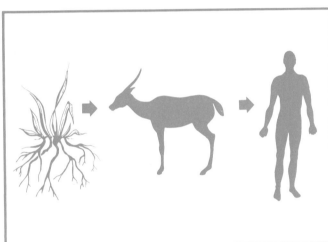

Fig 1.q

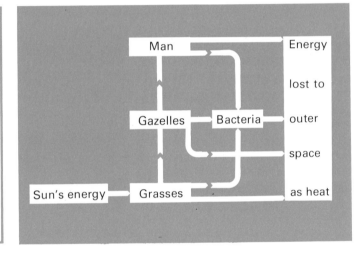

Fig 1.s

Habitat unity

Structure

We believe that no other planet in the solar system has habitats which allow human life to survive. Other planets possess neither the right 'ingredients' nor the conditions necessary for the growth and renewal of living things.

The 'ingredients' of life on earth are water, minerals and air. The transfer of these non-living forms of matter to the living world is made by green plants. These take ABIOTIC substances from water, air and weathered rock (in the soil or in ocean sediments) and trap the sun's energy to create living matter. The process by which they achieve this is PHOTOSYNTHESIS (fig. 1.p).

The living matter formed by plants can then be used by animals and man. The nutrients and energy absorbed by plants is passed along a chain of living things, first to herbivores and then to carnivores. The FOOD CHAIN in fig 1.a can be shown in diagrammatic form, fig 1.q.

Thus man is the third link along the food chain and is dependent on the efficiency of the photosynthesis of the grasses, the grazing of the antelope and his own hunting skill, PREDATION, for his survival. The efficiency of these processes is in turn dependent upon the availability of nutrients and energy and upon the conditions, such as temperature and wind, in which the plants and animals live.

Function: the renewal of life

Chemical energy does not build up without interruption in grasses, antelopes and men. Ultimately they die, and bacteria of decay break the once-living substances down into 'a drop of water, a puff of gas (CO_2) and a pinch of mineral salts[1]'. These are then available once more for incorporation into new living things. Thus nutrients are cycled from the non-living world, through the living world and back again to the non-living world (fig 1.r).

Energy, on the other hand, passes through plants and animals and is ultimately lost to outer space as heat (fig 1.s).

Thus that part of the earth where life exists, the BIOSPHERE, is a living system, an ECOSYSTEM, consisting of 'an ordered and highly integrated community of plants and animals together with the environment that influences it[2]'.

[1]Quoted in: J. Tivy, *Biogeography*, Oliver and Boyd, 1973
[2]'Biogeography in the sixth form': a report by the Geographical Association's standing committee for matters of mutual concern to sixth-form and university teachers; *Geography*, July 1975

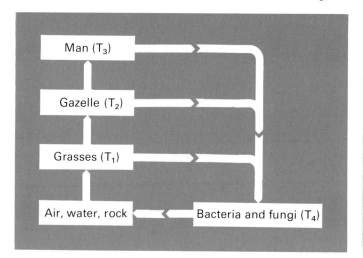

Fig 1.t

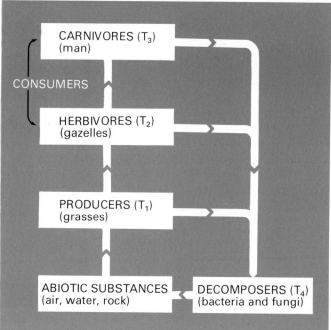

Fig 1.u

Equilibrium or change

Any one alteration in the balance of nature—in the supply of nutrients or energy, or in the conditions of a plant or animal—can trigger off a chain reaction throughout the whole of the habitat. The removal of water from the Saharan habitat caused the death of the vegetation, which in turn caused the death of the animals grazing on it and finally the death of man or his retreat from that part of the Sahara (see p. 8 and fig 1.n). Ultimately a new state of balance or equilibrium is reached. The relationships between the components of the earth's habitats are very intricate. Man, in trying to control his habitat, has been ignorant of its complex structure, and so of how wide-reaching might be the ultimate results of his interference.

To make a full study of an ecosystem we need to ask the following questions.
(i) *Structure* What is its structure and how is it organized?
(ii) *Function* How does it function in terms of
   (a) energy
   (b) nutrients
   (c) conditions
   (d) population interactions?
(iii) *Equilibrium* What degree of stability does it have?
(iv) *Change* How did it evolve? How might it develop in the future?

exercises

1.18 Categorize the habitats around your school or home according to the degree of man's alteration of them (as in exercise 1.3).

1.19 Find several man–land relationships in your locality which have changed through time, and try to explain them in terms of either man's culture or man's technology.

A closer look at ecosystems

Structure

Fig 1.r is a MODEL or abstraction of reality: it selects from, simplifies and orders a complex situation in an attempt to describe how the real world functions. The model links all the parts of the biosphere into a system and shows how it is organized in order to work. There are many other models, systems or concepts of the real world which help to explain how things function: for instance, the diagram of the hot-water system of a house, or the map of London's Underground railway.

Fig 1.t is a more abstract diagram of a system. It consists of compartments and flows, with arrows showing the

direction of flow through the system. In the food chain in fig 1.q, three compartments are necessary, starting with the grasses, before man gets his food. Each of these compartments is called a TROPHIC (food) level and is numbered according to its position in the chain: for example, grasses are at trophic level 1, T_1, gazelles at trophic level 2, T_2

Living things can also be classified according to the way they obtain their food (fig. 1.u). Plants manufacture their own from inorganic materials and are called PRODUCERS, or AUTOTROPHS or self-feeders. Animals are dependent on plants or other animals for food and are CONSUMERS, or HETEROTROPHS or other-feeders. These are of two kinds: for example, the gazelle is a vegetarian or herbivore, and man is a meat-eater or carnivore. The bacteria and fungi which break down plants and animals into their constituent inorganic chemicals are called DECOMPOSERS. These components—abiotic substances, producers, consumers and decomposers—are common to all ecosystems. This structure can be applied to any part of the earth, at any scale from a garden to a continent or to the whole earth itself.

ECOLOGICAL NICHES
Each plant or animal has a role to play in the functioning of an ecosystem: together they constitute the means by which chemical energy is transferred through the system. Those playing the same role are said to occupy parallel ECOLOGICAL NICHES. For instance, an antelope in Africa, a bison in North America and a kangaroo in Australia all, as herbivores, occupy parallel ecological niches.

exercises

1.20 Draw system diagrams, with compartments and flows, for the following sets of abiotic substances, plants and animals. First sort out the non-living and living components and place them in their correct order. Mark the direction of flow with arrows. Then state which animals fulfil the same ecological role as the Eskimo in (i).

(i) Water, Eskimo, air, lemming, soil, dwarf willow, arctic grouse, bacteria of decay.

(ii) Shark, phytoplankton, carbon dioxide, herring, ocean sediments, bacteria of decay, water, zooplankton.

(iii) Eagle, reeds, water, vole, air, soil, bacteria of decay, weasel.

The more diverse the species in a habitat, the more stable it is: that is, it contains more niches, each one occupied by an ecological specialist, which transfers energy through the system.

Function

ENERGY

Energy to 'drive' the ecosystem is derived from the sun. Plants during photosynthesis take in only 1% of the total light reaching the ground. As it passes through the system, energy is lost as heat at each trophic level. This is because

(i) the consumer does not eat all parts of the plant or animal, such as bones, teeth and fur;

(ii) heat is given off during bodily functions, such as tissue respiration;

(iii) some of the energy taken in is not used by the animal, but excreted.

Thus there is a scaling down of energy as it passes up the food chain in the ratio of plants 100: herbivores 10: carnivores 1.

Why do you think most food chains are limited to four or five links?

Almost all energy is ultimately changed to heat and is lost to outer space. It is *not* recycled. There is a THROUGHPUT OF ENERGY in an ecosystem.

NUTRIENTS

The various chemical elements of which the earth is composed enter the ecosystem by photosynthesis, combine to form living matter, circulate through the system, and then return to their reservoirs. There are two types of cycle: GASEOUS, such as the nitrogen

cycle, where the main reservoir is the air; and SEDIMENTARY, such as the phosphorus cycle, where the main reservoir is rocks.

exercises

1.21 Suggest another example of each type of nutrient cycle.

1.22 Write a page on how man has influenced
(i) the nitrogen cycle and
(ii) the phosphorus cycle. (Figs 1.v and 1.w.)

1.23 Under what circumstances could the phosphates lost to deep sediments be once more available to terrestrial ecosystems?

1.24 Do you think the cycling of nitrogen is faster or slower than that of phosphorus? Why?

CONDITIONS

Conditions controlling rates of photosynthesis are given on p. 25.

INTERACTIONS

These are determined by the size of the population at each trophic level and the reaction of the population of one trophic level on the previous one.

The flows between compartments are caused by the processes at work, and the process rates determine the levels of biomass in the compartments. This is analogous to a sink's being filled with water from a tap and at the same time emptied through an outflow pipe.

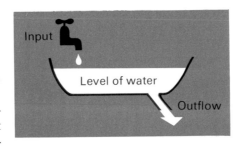

The levels of biomass at each trophic level vary through time and are determined by an intricate and delicately balanced network of cycles and reactions.

(i) the rate of flow of energy;
(ii) the rate of flow of nutrients;
(iii) environmental conditions, e.g. temperature, windiness;

(iv) the interactions between the trophic levels.

Levels and Rates

The *quantity* of living matter at each trophic level is called the BIOMASS and, to facilitate comparisons between different environments, is measured in grammes of dry matter per square metre. Because of the loss of energy and matter on the way up the food chain, the biomass of trophic levels forms a pyramid (see fig 1.x).

The *rate* of productivity of plants, their PRIMARY PRODUCTIVITY, is the

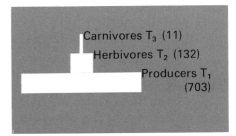

Carnivores T_3 (11)
Herbivores T_2 (132)
Producers T_1 (703)

Fig 1.x

basis of the whole ecosystem. It can be measured in various ways, the simplest being in grammes of dry matter per square metre per year.

exercises

Look at fig 1.y and answer the following questions.

1.25 What would happen to the level of the producer biomass if
(i) the rate of photosynthesis was the same as the rate of grazing?
(ii) the rate of grazing exceeded the rate of photosynthesis?

1.26 In the summer of 1976, environmental conditions favoured greenfly and they increased enormously in numbers.
(i) Described the effects this had *initially* on rose leaves eaten by the greenfly and on ladybirds preying on greenfly.
(ii) Say what happened *ultimately* when the greenflies' food supply decreased and their predators increased in number?

This mechanism of population control is called ECOLOGICAL REGULATION or the balance of nature.

1.27 Consider the following list and, for each activity, state which limiting factor—energy, nutrients, conditions of existence such as temperature, or population interactions—has been significantly altered by man. Try to give examples of some of the consequences he has brought about. Some answers may be debatable.

(i) Cutting out sunlight by air pollution.

(ii) Irrigating dry areas.

(iii) Vastly increasing human populations in the second and third trophic levels.

(iv) Killing parasites in large numbers.

(v) Dumping sewage in the seas.

(vi) Causing the extinction of certain animals.

(vii) Using greenhouses.

(viii) Increasing the numbers of domestic animals.

(ix) Leaching nutrients from the soil.

(x) Continuously cropping the land.

(xi) Burning fossil fuels and increasing the carbon-dioxide content of the atmosphere.

(xii) Introducing animals to a foreign environment, e.g. cats in coral atolls.

(xiii) Introducing new chemical substances such as herbicides.

(xiv) Applying fertilisers to the soil.

1.28 Suggest some of the consequences of the following.

(i) The death of green plants over the whole of the earth's surface (read *Death of Grass* by John Christopher, Sphere, 1978).

(ii) The earth moving further from the sun.

(iii) The earth stopping spinning on its axis.

(iv) The removal of soil from a farmer's land.

(v) The emission of herbicidal gas over a hay field.

129. Try to design a self-sustaining life support system to enable man to live on the moon. It might help to debate this first and then vote on the most feasible plan. Bear in mind the following points.

(i) Some abiotic substances are absent from the moon and would need to be transported there initially.

(ii) The cycling of nutrients should be described in detail and care taken to avoid loss of nut-rients from the ecosystem.

(iii) Remember the relationship of the moon to the supplier of energy.

(iv) Lunar conditions such as temperature, gravity and spin are different from those on earth.

(v) Ecosystems based on water instead of land could be devised.

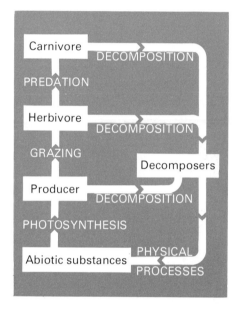

Fig 1.y

Fig 1.v

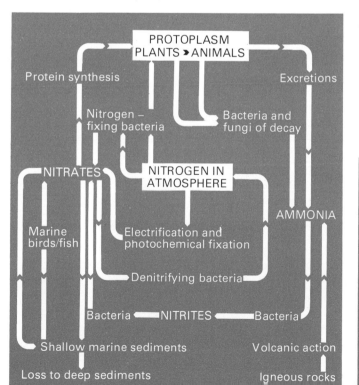

Fig 1.w

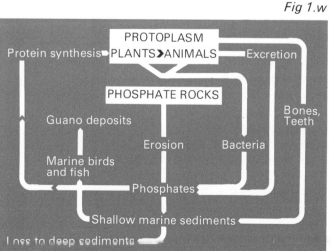

2. Clothing the earth: colonization and plant succession

Surtsey

Newly formed volcanic islands are wonderful 'laboratories' for the scientist. He can observe, measure and record the processes of nature at work there today and so find the key to larger-scale patterns of nature established elsewhere long ago.

On the 14th Nov 1963 a volcanic eruption started in the sea to the south of Iceland, and an island gradually built up, 2.5 square km in area and 172 m high. This island, called Surtsey (fig 2.a) is half covered in lava, the rest mostly ashes—tephra—hardening into tuff and beaches of sand and gravel. The colonization of this virgin island by plants and animals (fig 2.b) has offered an almost unprecedented opportunity for scientific study.

exercises

2.1 Read the following extract and study table 2.c.[1] Then write on the colonization, soil development, ecosystem and plant succession of Surtsey, using the guidelines in exercise 2.2–2.4.

'My first visit to the island took place ... six months after the eruption started, at which time various strains of bacteria and a few moulds were collected on agar plates, one fly was found, while a few seagulls, waders and a snow bunting were seen. In addition, a few plant parts and seeds of various beach and sand plants had drifted upon the eastern shore ...' (p. 3).

'Similarly, spores of ferns, mosses and lichens will be able to disperse by wind. However, seeds of vascular plants equipped with plumes for wind dispersal have also been noted. Once a shower of small fruits of the common groundsel came drifting on the air like an invasion of parachutists. These fruits very likely came from the mainland. ... Similarly, in the autumn of 1971 and again in 1972 there was an airborne invasion of the nuts of cotton grass. ... Only the light seeds and those equipped with bristles for the purpose will be conveyed in this way to the island ...' (p. 58).

'Sea-gulls are constantly soaring above Surtsey and various sea-birds inhabit or visit the island. ... The birds which have now started to nest on

Surtsey will probably carry plant material to their nesting grounds. ... Their nests will then serve as incubation areas for various smaller organisms which will enjoy shelter, heat, and the fertile soil provided by the birds. These spots will become colonization centres for such organisms. Some of the migratory birds caught on Surtsey have had parasites, both in their alimentary tract as well as on the exterior of their body. Beetles have been discovered in their throats and these in turn may also host parasites. Some of these organisms may spread among the local bird population and become inhabitants ...' (p. 66).

'On Surtsey bacteria, moulds, algae and vascular plants were discovered before any moss or lichens were observed. Three years passed until moss started to grow on the lava, and it was only during the eighth year that the lichens started to colonize.

'A wide variety of blue-green algae have been collected on Surtsey ... but they cannot be considered of major ecological importance in the develop-

ment of life on Surtsey' (p. 90).

'Different microzoa were discovered. ... These animals are all capable of withstanding severe environmental changes such as drought and frost. It is therefore clear that they are capable of being the pioneer consumers at the lower trophic level of the food chain in the moist lava habitat on Surtsey, where they feed on the blue-green algae and bacteria.

'The environment on Surtsey is cool, windy and rainy, but the periodical drought is mostly responsible for the slow establishment of life on the island. As the tephra gradually hardens into tuff, its water-retention will increase' (p. 177).

'The presence of sea-gulls on the island also greatly affects the future soil of Surtsey by their excreta supplying fertilizer, containing both minerals and organic matter. ... Despite the precipitation being quite high, no rainwater accumulates in any amount on the island but seeps right through the

[1] S. Fridriksson, *Surtsey. Evolution of life on a volcanic island*, Butterworth, 1975

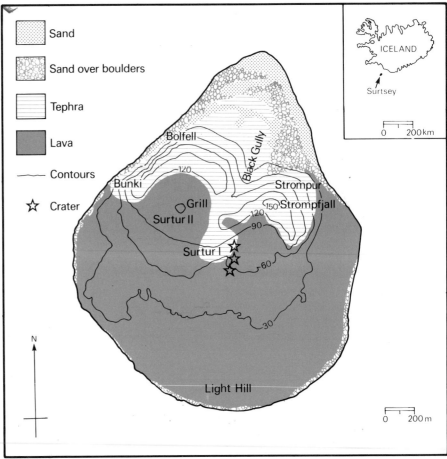

Fig 2.a

Fig 2.b

Table 2.c Plant and animal species recorded on Surtsey between 1965 and 1973

Date	Number of moss species	lichen species	algal species	vascular plants	insects	Biomass of vegetation dry gm/m²
1965				23	8	
1966				5	22	
1967	2			51	63	
1968	6		100	114	71	
1969	7		x	63	135	
1970	18	1	x	101	135	
1971	40	x	x	83	x	0.518
1972	66	x	x	199	x	3.076
1973	x	11	160	1273	x	3.412

Biomass is the quantity of living matter present, expressed in grammes of dry matter per unit area.

x: no information available.

porous substrates, whether it is of lava, tephra or sand' (p. 127).

'It may be assumed that the Surtsey moss will develop a thick continuous carpet, at least in the centre of the lava apron. This moss carpet will then collect dust and minerals, and nutrients will be deposited in the dead mat of moss rhizoids which will form a layer of humus in the juvenile soil. The accumulation of humus will then cause moisture to be retained on the lava surface. The pioneer lichens will occupy the higher ridges of the lava and gradually corrode its surface, providing better anchorage for other plants. This primary succession of moss and lichen will provide a suitable habitat for higher plants which then, in turn, will invade the lava area. Gradually a heath vegetation with sedge, crowberry and low-growing willows may invade the moss carpet in the most sheltered areas. But it is highly unlikely that the island will ever obtain a climax vegetation of birch as the lava flows of the mainland, because of the frequent salt spray and the heavy storms' (p. 178).

'So far there has not been a great deal of organic matter produced by the terrestrial vegetation on Surtsey, and the producers have thus not been able to support any substantial amount of life occupying higher trophic levels. Most of the animals observed on Surtsey are, therefore, visitors that obtain their energy from sources not directly belonging to the island's ecosystem' (p. 121).

exercises

Colonization

2.2 Describe the location, size and date of formation of the island.

2.3 Where do the colonizing plants and animals come from?

2.4 Give three ways in which plants reach the island, apart from being introduced accidentally by man.

2.5 List the first plants to reach the island.

2.6 What was the plant cover like after
(i) three years;
(ii) eight years;
(iii) ten years?

2.7 List the animals mentioned on the island so far, under three headings:
(i) visitors;
(ii) partial occupants;
(iii) permanent occupants.

2.8 Discuss the importance of birds to the colonization of Surtsey.

2.9 Why is the colonization of the island so slow?

Soil development

2.10 Name the three types of parent material from which the soil develops.

2.11 Describe the early stages of soil formation and comment upon
(i) weathering of rock;
(ii) addition of nutrients and humus;
(iii) development of water retention.

Ecosystem

2.12 Comment on the biomass of the vegetation between 1971 and 1973. Compare these figures with those of an island close by, called Heimaey, where in 1972 the average biomass was 906.1 dry grammes per square metre. Heimaey is covered with meadowland, heath vegetation and puffin-ground vegetation.

2.13 Why, up to now, are the food chains on Surtsey so limited?

2.14 What is the present main energy source for the animals?

2.15 What happens to the energy from the sun which reaches the surface?

2.16 Describe Surtsey's environmental conditions (CLIMATIC and EDAPHIC).

2.17 Describe the supply of nutrients and water to the ecosystem.

2.18 Is competition between plants, and between plants and animals, important at this stage in the development of the ecosystem?

2.19 Why is the island's ecosystem so unstable?

2.20 Will it become more stable in the future? Why?

Plant succession

2.21 How does Fridriksson see the vegetation developing in the future?

2.22 How will the mosses and lichens provide a suitable habitat for the heath vegetation which will take their place?

2.23 Why will birch trees not succeed the heath vegetation?

2.24 What happens to the number of plant and animal species through time?

Fig 2.f

Krakatoa

Studies similar to those of Surtsey were made of Krakatoa (fig 2.d), an island in the Sunda Strait between Java and Sumatra, which erupted in 1883. Scientists visited it three years after the eruption and by then thirty species of plants had established themselves. Ten years later the island was covered with savanna and isolated shrubs; and scientists estimated that 60% of the species had been transported by sea, 32% by air currents and 8% by birds. Twenty-five years after the eruption the island was covered with a thick forest and had an animal population similar to that of the neighbouring islands. (Table 2.e.) The colonization of Krakatoa was rapid because of its high humidity and temperatures, and because of the rapid weathering of the lava to form a rich soil.

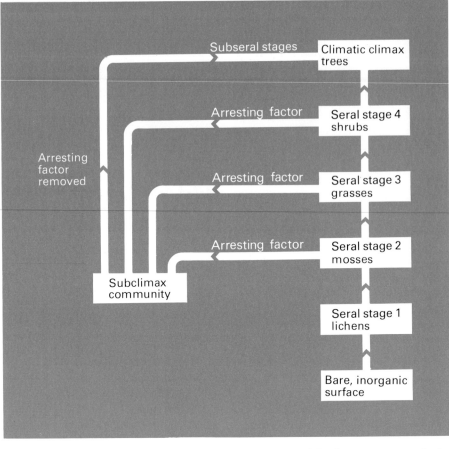

Table 2.e Number of species on Krakatoa

	1908	1921	1933
Flowering plants	103	142	219
Vascular crypto- grams	12	42	52
Mosses	—	19	—
Total species of animals	200	618	795

Plant succession

Studies such as these show that, after colonization, the process of vegetation change, the PLANT SUCCESSION, follows the same general pattern. A series of plant communities occupies the area through time; at each SERAL STAGE, the plant community helps the development of the soil, making it deeper and richer and improving its water-retaining properties. It also creates conditions of protection, shelter and anchorage which favour the next community of plants, which will be taller, more aggressive and demanding than its predecessor. Each community thus creates conditions which enable the next community to oust its predecessor because it can compete more successfully for light, nutrients and water.

Thus, on bare rocky surfaces, the first seral stage consists of lichens which can withstand drought for long periods and make use of water as soon as it is available. The lichens etch away par-ticles of rock and help soil development not only by aiding weathering but also by contributing small amounts of organic material after death. A water-retaining layer develops over the rock, the habitat is less susceptible to drought and conditions are created for takeover, usually by mosses, as the second seral stage. These, in turn, add to the nutrient store in the soil and deepen it so that grasses can take over. The final seral stages in this development are low-growing shrubs and then trees. Thus there is a progression from simple to more complex vegetation, from one layer of plants to several layers and from an unstable to a more stable plant community. The number of species of animals, as of plants, increases through the succession; so does the productivity of the communities.

Climatic climax vegetation

Ultimately the vegetation develops to the most diverse and complex possible for the environment and remains stable. In theory it is in balance with the climate and soil, in a steady state: the inputs of energy and nutrients are in balance with the outputs, and the species composition is stable, with birth and death rates in balance. In practice, however, environmental conditions are usually not stable long enough for this to happen.

The final seral stage is called the CLIMATIC CLIMAX VEGETATION. The length of time taken to reach the climax varies widely, depending on the nature of the parent material, and of the dispersal of plants and animals, and also on the conditions of relief and climate. Sometimes the vegetation does not develop through to its climax, because of an arresting factor such as too-steep slopes or too-marshy conditions which inhibit soil or plant development. In theory Surtsey's climatic climax vegetation should be silver-birch woodland, but salt spray and heavy storms will inhibit tree growth, and Fridriksson forecasts that the vegetation will be held at the heath stage. This arrested stage is called a SUBCLIMAX. Generally, if the arresting factor is removed, vegetation continues through a series of sub-seral stages to its climax (fig 2.f).

Sometimes, as on Krakatoa in 1883,

Fig 2.d   Fig 2.g

the climax vegetation is suddenly displaced, leaving a bare surface, and if natural processes are allowed to operate, a series of subseral stages will occupy the area until the climatic climax vegetation is restored.

Sometimes man, by regular firing or grazing of the land, interferes with the succession and holds the vegetation steady at what is called a PLAGIO-CLIMAX. Moorlands in the British Isles are examples of this. If the influence of man is removed, the vegetation will revert through a series of subseral stages to the climatic climax vegetation (fig 2.g). This is called SECONDARY SUCCESSION and is usually more rapid than successions starting from bare surfaces, as the soil which has already formed is rich in nutrients and retains water.

A great variety of bare inorganic surfaces are constantly being exposed today, although they form only a tiny proportion of the earth's surface. They include natural ones such as mud flats, sand dunes, areas abandoned by shrinking glaciers or created by flooding, river erosion or land-slides; and man-made ones include old slag-heaps, quarries, derelict land, and abandoned roads, railway lines, airfields, building sites and farmland.

exercises

2.25 Try to find such an area and make the following observations and recordings.[1]

Fieldwork

2.26 Find out how long ago the surface was laid bare.

2.27 Describe the structure and composition of the parent material in as much detail as possible.

2.28 Describe the soil or rudimentary soil: e.g. depth, colour, texture, pH, water-retaining properties, weathering of parent material, root depth and inputs from vegetation.

2.29 Describe the conditions of the ecosystem: e.g. exposure (windiness), temperatures, angle of slope, aspect, and any specialized conditions such as saltiness on sand dunes, chemicals on tips, air pollution.

2.30 Observe any adaptations of the vegetation to withstand harsh environmental conditions.

2.31 Describe the percentage cover and percentage frequency of the vegetation, using up to four types of quadrat to up to four layers of vegetation: $\frac{1}{2}$ metre $\times$ $\frac{1}{2}$ metre for the moss layer, 1 metre $\times$ 1 metre for the grass layer, 4 metre $\times$ 4 metre for the shrub layer and 10 metre $\times$ 10 metre for the tree layer.

2.32 If possible, remove one square metre of vegetation, dry and weigh to give some idea of bio-mass. *You should only attempt this in areas such as abandoned building sites where the environment will not be defaced.*

2.33 Suggest the stage of plant suc-cession reached in the area you have studied and refer to:
(i) the proportion of bare ground;
(ii) the number of plant species;
(iii) the number of plant layers;
(iv) the efficiency of the ecosystem: e.g. the percentage plant cover and the probable proportion of the sun's energy entering the ecosystem via the plants;
(v) soil development and limitations of nutrient and water supply;
(vi) the stability of the present ecosystem;
(vii) the probable development of vegetation in the future as a result of plant competition and changing habitat conditions.

2.34 Try to find an area close by abandoned for a longer or shorter time than the area studied and compare them.

2.35 Visit the same area each year and note the changes.

[1] Soil study is described on pages 37–46. Details of the instruments and field methods used are given in: Rona Mottershead, 'Practical Biogeography', *Teaching Geography*, no. 23, Geographical Association, Sheffield, 1974

Fig 2.h

Plant successions in different environments: examples from Britain

Parkgate

Parkgate, on the Dee estuary, near Chester, was once a thriving port. In 1742 Handel embarked from this quay (fig 2.h) for Dublin to hear the first performance of his *Messiah*. Today forty-nine square kilometres of the former estuary are classified as dry land (fig 2.j).

Compare figs 2.h and 2.j, and then fig 2.k.

2.36 Comment on the percentage cover of plants in figs 2.l–p.

2.37 Discuss the efficiency of the three ecosystems in terms of utilization of the sun's energy.

2.38 Explain why there are different species at each seral stage.

2.39 Account for the change in height of the plants at each seral stage.

2.40 Why does the number of species increase through time?

2.41 Comment on the rate of progression of seral change.

2.42 Today much of the marsh is grazed by sheep. What effect will this have on seral development?

A PLANT SUCCESSION IN A SALTWATER ENVIRONMENT IS CALLED A *HALOSERE*.

Fig 2.k   *Fig 2.j*

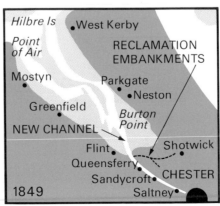

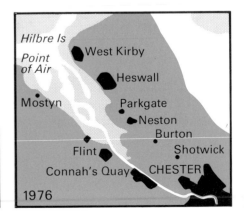

Fig 2.l

Today in some parts, sea meadow grass, sea asters, scurvy grass and sea purslane form a dense carpet of salt marsh (fig 2.n).

Spartina grass (fig 2.l) and glasswort (fig 2.m) are the main pioneer species of the mud and are able to withstand inundation by the sea and the saline conditions.

Fig 2.n

On the older, drier marshes are sea milkwort, sea arrow grass, the common reed, sea club-rush and southern marsh orchid (fig 2.p). At this stage, inundation by the sea is only at spring tides, and therefore salinity is lower and the substratum less mobile that at either of the two previous stages.

Fig 2.m

Fig 2.p

19

Ainsdale sand dunes, Lancashire coast

As one plant community ousts its predecessor (see p. 16), the soil, micro-climatic conditions and animals dependent on the vegetation also change. At Ainsdale lines of sand dunes run roughly north to south at a slight angle to the coast (fig 2.q). The most recently formed dunes are on the west, closest to the seashore; the older dunes, probably formed a few hundred years ago, lie to the east. The dunes are represented diagrammatically in fig 2.r, with details of soil, animal life and plants from a transect across the dunes.

Marram grass helps to stabilize dunes (fig 2.s). Queen Elizabeth I recognized its usefulness and made it a criminal offence to uproot it. It thrives on freshly blown sand, trapping it by interrupting the wind with its tall,

sharp shoots. It can grow up through accumulating sand in the extremely harsh, windy environment of the dunes, where nutrient levels are low, water retention is poor and alkaline content is high because of the shelly fragments in the sand. The network of roots and underground stems it leaves behind helps to stabilize the dune.

exercises

2.43 Look at figs 2.t–v and identify the four sites of fig 2.r.

2.44 Look at the soils at the four sites, and describe and account for their development. Give reasons for the differences in pH.

2.45 Comment on the number of plant species at each of the four sites. Why are there fewer species at site 4 than at site 3?

2.46 Comment on the lengths of the food chains.

2.47 Compare the efficiency and stability of the ecosystems at sites 2 and 3.

2.48 Site 4 is a subclimax. Why is the succession arrested here? If the arresting factor were removed, the succession would probably be as shown in fig 2.w.

2.49 Man, the farmer, has removed the woodland climax from much of Britain and created many of the conditions of the pioneer stage in his farmland. In what ways does arable farmland resemble the pioneer stage of plant succession?

A PLANT SUCCESSION IN A SANDY ENVIRONMENT IS CALLED A *PSAMMOSERE*.

Fig 2.q   Fig 2.w

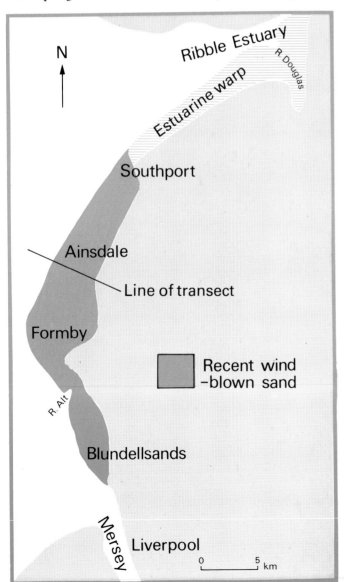

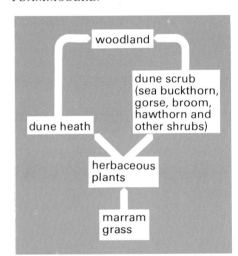

Fig 2.s

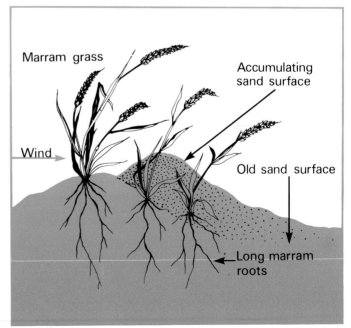

Fig 2.t   Fig 2.u    Fig 2.v

Fig 2.r

	Shore and foredunes 1	Mobile dune 2	Fixed dune 3	Dune heath 4
Soil	Unconsolidated sand with shelly fragments. No organic content. No water retention.	Sand with traces of humic material. Fewer shells than 1. No water retention.	Brown surface humic layer 8cm deep, overlying sand. No visible shells. Some water retention.	Black, humus-rich surface layer 30cm deep. Water retentive, overlying light grey layer 10cm deep, overlying orange sand
pH	8	8	5	4
% cover bare ground	100	85	10	0
Number of plant species observed	1	seaward side 5 leeside 15	27	12
Main plants and their frequency	sea couch grass 1	marram grass 90 red fescue 85	sand sedge 75 Yorkshire fog and other grasses 70 marram grass 60 red fescue 60 creeping willow 60 dewberry 55	ling heather 90 gorse 10 heath rush 30
Main animal species	visitors which are part of maritime ecosystem e.g. gulls, oystercatchers	skylark ringed plover common lizard (few animal species)	six spot burnett moth shelduck meadow pipit sand lizard	wood mouse field vole common shrew rabbit kestrel

Hatchmere and Flaxmere

Hatchmere, in Delamere Forest, Cheshire, occupies a kettle-hole formed 10 000 years ago by retreating ice sheets. Today this freshwater lake is gradually being infilled, and a number of distinctive vegetational zones can be seen around its shores, representing stages in plant succession. (Figs 2.x and 2.ab.)

These zones may be studied in detail by means of a transect at right angles to the shore. Readings were made at Hatchmere of the percentage cover of the various plant species in one-metre quadrats; these were taken at five-metre intervals along a line stretching from the shrub belt about eighty metres from the shore to a point within the lake itself, near the limit of vegetation. The readings are in fig 2.z.

exercises

2.50 (i) Plot on graph paper twelve bar charts, one above the other, to show the percentage cover of each plant species. Plot them in list order. Make the base line proportional to the length of the transect and draw in the columns one small square in width at the appropriate points on the line of transect. Take one large square of graph paper along the vertical axis to represent 100% cover.

(ii) Colour each column according to the categories in table 2.y. Use blue for set I, yellow for II, green for III and brown for IV.

(iii) Describe and comment on your findings.

2.51 (i) Here is an alternative method of using the data in table 2.y. Sketch in the plants on your copy of fig 2.z. Eight plants are marked with symbols. On each vertical line of the cross-section, draw the appropriate symbols, showing their relative size, for the plants that occur there.

(ii) Try to describe and explain the development of the vegetation and link your explanation to the accumulation of sediments shown on the cross-section. Do you notice anything about the size of the plants?

(iii) Suggest a series of vegetation zones characterized by the main plants of each zone and their conditions of growth.

2.52 If there is a suitable lake near your school, carry out a similar survey of your own. In addition to recording the vegetation, you could also test the pH of the sediments at various stages along your transect.

Fig 2.ab

Fig 2.x

Fig 2.aa

Fig 2.z

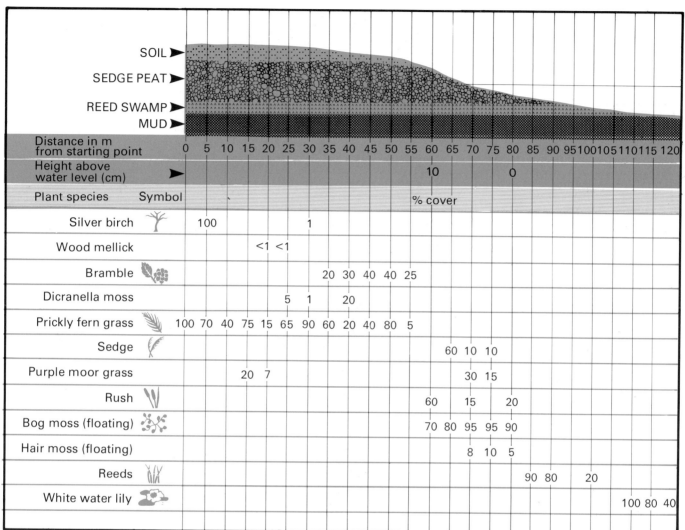

2.53 If you have a peat borer or coring tool, sample the sediments in the swampy area close to the lake and from your findings infer the vegetational changes that have occurred.

2.54 Try to find old maps or old photographs of lakes near your home to investigate vegetational changes over the last hundred years.

Flaxmere is close to Hatchmere (figs 2.aa and 2.ab). Here the open-water surface has been completely covered by vegetation. The plant succession has progressed further than at Hatchmere, and silver-birch scrub has taken over in some parts of the former lake.

2.55 What type of woodland do you think may succeed the silver birch?

A PLANT SUCCESSION IN A FRESHWATER ENVIRONMENT IS CALLED A *HYDROSERE*.

Table 2.y Conditions and characteristic plant species of zones in freshwater lakes

Zone	Conditions	Characteristic plant species
I	Shallow, translucent, open water. Very low nutrient levels. Clay mud. Problem of aeration.	White water lilies (*Nymphaea alba*)
II	Shallower water with higher nutrient levels. Some peat deposited. Very poor aeration.	Bur-reeds (*Sparganium*) Common reed (*Phragmites australis*) Reed mace (*Typha latifolia*) Water celery (*Apium nodiflorum*) Yellow flag (*Iris Pseudacorus*)
III	Acid boggy conditions. Water rich in nutrients. Peat accumulation.	Bog moss (*Sphagnum*) Hair moss (*Polytrichum*)
IV	A true soil developing, poorly drained but better aerated than in the other three zones.	Rush (*Juncus*) Sedge (*Carex*) Prickly fern grass (*Agrostic tenuis*) Purple moor grass (*Molinia*) Wavy hair grass (*Deschampsia flexuosa*) Wood melick (*Melica uniflora*) Bramble (*Rubus fruticosa*) Alder (*Alnus*) Birch (*Betula*)

Fig 2.ac

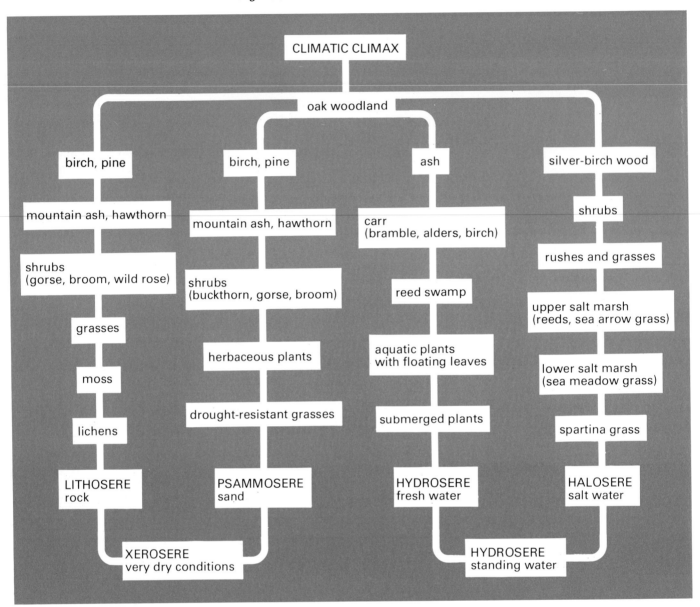

Lithosere, Psammosere, Halosere and Hydrosere

Plant successions may start in either very dry conditions (XEROSERES) or very wet conditions. (HYDROSERES). Xeroseres are further categorized into LITHOSERES (bare rock), as on Surtsey; and PSAMMOSERES (bare sand), as at Ainsdale. Hydroseres are further categorized into HALOSERES (saltwater), as at Parkgate; and HYDROSERES (freshwater), as at Hatchmere. The lithosere develops from bare rock, as on Surtsey, and it is difficult to study at school level, as its progression is very slow. Fig 2.ac summarizes the four types of succession. In theory all types of plant succession under similar climatic conditions in the British Isles should converge towards a similar climax type of vegetation: that is, oak woodland.

However, the idea of climatic climax is theoretical, as conditions of climate and soil rarely remain constant; moreover human activities have changed most of the earth's natural vegetation, creating either plagioclimax vegetation or replacing natural vegetation altogether with agricultural systems.

exercises

2.56 Contrast, in general terms, the pioneer stage of a succession with the climatic climax. Refer to:
(i) the percentage cover of bare surface;
(ii) the percentage cover of plants;
(iii) species diversity;
(iv) adaptations of species;
(v) the height and strata of the plant communities;
(vi) biomass;
(vii) soil development: e.g. depth, water retention, organic content;
(viii) the functioning of the two systems in terms of nutrients, water and energy;
(ix) the efficiency, productivity and stability of the two systems.

2.57 Discuss the statement, 'the process of succession itself is biological, not physical. That is, the physical environment determines the pattern of succession but does not cause it[1]'.

[1]E. P. Odum, *Ecology*, Holt, Rinehart and Winston, 2nd ed., 1975, p. 151

3 Patterns of plant growth and their causes

If you look at the patterns of plant growth in a plot about ten metres by twenty metres in your garden or park, you will find a great variation in vigour as each plant responds to complex micro-influences in its environment.

exercises

3.1 Make a plan of your plot and mark on it areas of growth in three categories: vigorous, moderate and poor.

3.2 Make a second plan, recording first the *physical* conditions of growth: exposed or sheltered from the wind, open or shady aspect, deep or shallow soil, alkaline or acid soil, well drained or badly drained, flat or sloping, subject to late frosts or fairly frost-free. If you have the necessary equipment, then record quantitative features: temperatures at various times during the day, hours of sunshine, hours of shade, pH, moisture content of the soil, weight of humic matter in the soil, angle of slope.

You may find variation in plant vigour even where there is very little variation in the physical conditions. This may be due to a second set of influences: the *biotic* ones. These influences include competition from other plants for light, water and nutrients, attack by insects or fungi or even by the family pet! The variation could also be due to the history of the garden: for instance where a fire had been lit, where previous crops had grown or where weeds had invaded from a plot next door.

Climax vegetation is also the result of all the interacting habitat factors. Table 3.a gives a comprehensive list. Scientists no longer believe that climate alone controls the type of climax. This old idea of MONOCLIMAX — coincidence of climatic and vegetation zones — was put forward in 1908 by an American naturalist called Frederick Clements (1874–1945). His idea has now been modified to the concept of POLYCLIMAX: the climax is not determined solely by climate but by the interaction of all the factors influencing plant growth. For example, the climax vegetation in Britain is beech woodland on softer limestones and sessile oak woodland on acid soils.

exercises

A desert in Britain

3.3 Look at fig 3.b, taken in the Keen of Hamar, Shetland Isles. Suggest at least five ways in which the area resembles part of the Saharan Desert. A biological desert is a region where plant and animal biomass is meagre and productivity low. This may be due to *any or all* of the following five major factors:
(i) lack of water;
(ii) lack of nutrients;

climate inhospitable, flat, no vegetation, poor soil

(iii) low energy inputs;
(iv) conditions adverse to growth: e.g. too low or too high temperatures; extreme wind; toxic substances in the soil, air or water; instability of the soil or anchorage;
(v) activities of a predator (including man).

3.4 Look at figs 3.c–e and the field notes about the climate and soils in the Keen of Hamar in Unst, Shetland. Suggest which of the limiting factors listed above are responsible for the desert here.

Fig 3.b

Table 3.a Factors affecting the distribution of plants

I PHYSICAL (permissive) FACTORS
Light
Temperature
Moisture
Soil conditions
Mineral nutrients (geology)
CO_2 in the atmosphere
Aspect

II BIOTIC (selective) FACTORS
A plant's range of tolerance
Plant dispersal and plant migration

Competition from other plants for	light
	water
	nutrients

Animals
Defoliating insects
Pathogenic fungus

Man	grazing animals
	using fire
	growing crops
	clearing vegetation
	causing the emission of toxic gases

The Keen of Hamar, Shetland: a field study

Site features
60° 48′ N, 50° W
In the paths of the Gulf Stream and weather systems from the Atlantic Ocean
Altitude—below 150 m
Terrain—fairly flat

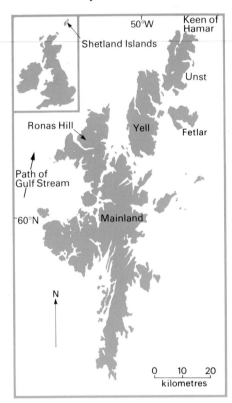

Fig 3.c

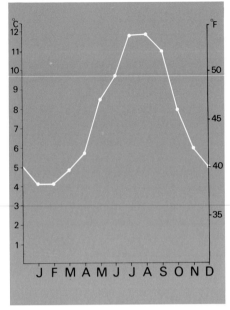

Fig 3.d

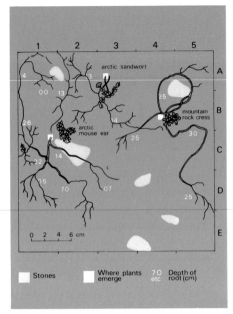

Fig 3.g

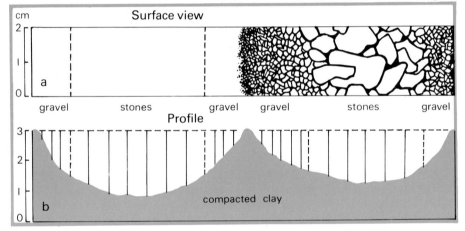

Fig 3.e

Climatic data
Mean monthly temperatures at Balta Sound nearby are shown in fig 3.d. Total annual rainfall is 1125mm. Rain falls in every month. Wettest months are November, December and January. Driest months are May and June. POTENTIAL WATER DEFICIT (the amount by which loss from potential evapotranspiration exceeds incoming precipitation) occurs only in three months—May, June and July—and is 33 mm per month. The area is snow-free. The mean relative humidity is the highest in Britain—80 to 85%. There is the highest concentration of salts in the air for any place in Europe. Wind speeds are very high, the average wind speed of Lerwick being 7.3 metres per second. Summer days are very long (13% longer than in central Scotland).

Soil observations
The soil is described as 'raw and skeletal'. No burning or grazing has occurred. The parent material is serpentine, which causes the soil to have a severe nutrient imbalance, being particularly deficient in phosphorus. There are also low levels of calcium, nitrogen and potassium and high concentrations of magnesium, chromium and nickel. The soil is highly mineral with very little organic content. Physical weathering is very intense. Frost shattering, frost heaving and solifluction occur. There is some striping of the soil. The soil has many angular stones 1 to 3 cm in diameter overlying finer material. The soil is very unstable because of frost heaving. Fig 3.e shows the nature of the soil stripes.

Plant detail
Plant cover varies between 1.5% and 20%. There are no trees. The vegetation consists mainly of low woody herbaceous perennials; 25 species are present, classified as arctic alpine. Mosses are scarce. Productivity is low, the yearly average being less than 1 dry gm/m² per day. Productivity during the short growing season is between 1 and 4 dry gm/m² per day.

Two typical species, arctic mouse ear and arctic sandwort, are shown in fig 3.f. Other arctic alpine species include stiff sedge, hoary whitlow grass, creeping cudweed and purple saxifrage. There are also a few low shrubs such as juniper and least willow.

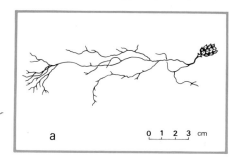

a

0 1 2 3 cm

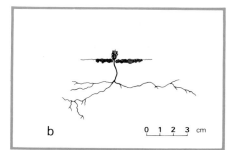

b

0 1 2 3 cm

Plant adaptations and tolerance
The plants on the Keen of Hamar are obviously tolerant of harsh edaphic and climatic conditions.

Fig 3.f

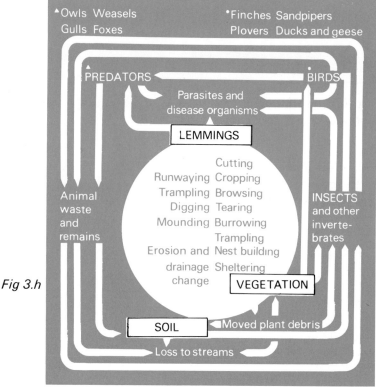

Fig 3.h

exercises

3.5 Write an account of the inter-relationships of climate, soil and vegetation on the Keen of Hamar and indicate how the plants are adapted to withstand the harsh conditions. Fig 3.g shows the root profiles of the arctic sandwort, mouse ear and mountain rock cress. The following questions may help you in your account.
(i) What is the distance apart of the shoots emerging from the soil?
(ii) Why are the roots so long and why do they vary in depth?
(iii) What is the top/root ratio of the plants? How do you explain this ratio?

3.6 Discuss the relative influences of soil and climate on the vegetation of the Keen of Hamar.

Arctic alpine vegetation is rare in Britain; it occurs on Ronas Hill on Unst and on the highest parts of the Scottish Grampians. Tiny patches grow on ledges in other mountain areas, for instance round Cwm Idwal in North Wales. If you do discover some of these rare patches, *please leave them undisturbed for other people to enjoy.*

3.7 Deep oceans are deserts: their productivity is below 0.5 dry gm/m² per day. Why are they deserts?

3.8 Find a patch of ground which is very sparsely vegetated or denuded of vegetation and decide which of the five factors listed in exercise 3.3 are responsible. Where are the man-made deserts in Britain today?

Are they spreading?

Deserts of the Arctic

Plants
In the arctic regions of North America, Greenland and Eurasia, tundra vegetation has much in common with that of the Keen of Hamar (see fig 1.e). It is characterized by low plants, under half a metre in height, with mainly VEGETATIVE REGENERATION (not seeding); plant cover and biological diversity are low, and although at times there is rapid daily growth, annual production is low (50 to 200 dry gm/m²/yr). The decomposition rate is slow and organic matter accumulates on the surface of the soil. Tundra plants also have a low top/root ratio.

The actual composition of the plant communities will, of course, vary with local conditions. There are no trees; mosses, lichens, grasses, sedges and herbaceous shrubs usually occur. The vegetation may be snow-covered for between two and four months, and for at least seven months, temperatures are below 0°C. Day length varies between 0 hours in the winter and 24 hours in the summer. The growing season is short and cool (usually less than three months). Below the shallow, active layer of soil lies a permanently frozen zone, the PERMAFROST, which may be up to five hundred metres deep. (See the description of soil on page 59.)

Animals
The low primary production supports a relatively low animal biomass, and there is a marked seasonal variation in annual numbers and productivity. Few animal species are tolerant of the harsh tundra conditions. Food chains are usually short. Snow prevents many vertebrates such as birds and caribou from inhabiting the tundra during winter. Insects overwinter in the tundra as eggs, larvae or pupae. Small mammals, such as hares, rodents and shrews, stay in burrows in the tundra, insulated by the snow. Fig 3.h shows the importance of small mammals to the ecosystem, and their interdependence with the soil and with the vegetation they need for food and shelter. (See exercise 3.9.)

Man has already had a considerable impact on tundra ecosystems by burning the vegetation and by grazing animals. His interference with these ecosystems is likely to increase markedly as he exploits minerals in the tundra. The opening-up of the oilfields in Alaska, for instance, has already prevented some animals from reaching their normal grazing lands, caused soil erosion and water pollution, and greatly reduced the area of wilderness. Many consider this a greedy act of large-scale vandalism.

exercises

3.9 Find further information for yourself on lemmings, and referring to fig 3.h, write an essay on the importance of lemmings to the maintenance of tundra ecosystems.

4 Woodlands

Fig 4.a

Fig 4.a shows that about two thirds of Britain's climax vegetation was oak woodland before man altered it; and that it occupied the best sites for vegetative growth. Today only tiny remnants of the oak woodland remain, and even these are not completely natural, having been replanted and managed by man.

exercises

4.1 Look at fig 4.a and sort the first ten items in the key into trees and non-trees. Name a location in Britain for each type.

4.2 Write a paragraph explaining the pattern of climatic climax vegetation in the British Isles.

4.3 Compare figs 4.a and 4.b.

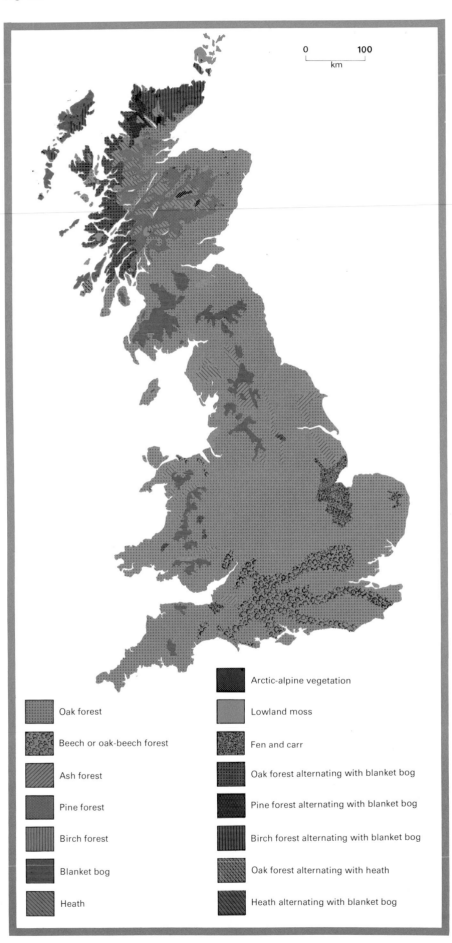

0   100
km

Arctic-alpine vegetation

Oak forest

Lowland moss

Beech or oak-beech forest

Fen and carr

Ash forest

Oak forest alternating with blanket bog

Pine forest

Pine forest alternating with blanket bog

Birch forest

Birch forest alternating with blanket bog

Blanket bog

Oak forest alternating with heath

Heath

Heath alternating with blanket bog

Fig 4.b

much peat moor

Molinia, sedges, etc, at low levels
Fescue-agrostis at high levels
Arctic-alpine vegetation at higher levels

N

mountain fescue
all round edges

0   100
km

Arctic-alpine vegetation

Heather moor and heather fell

Heaths of the New Forest type

Fescue-agrostis grassland and
mountain fescue (acid grassland)

Nardus and nardus-fescue moor
(dry grass moor)

Peat moor and cotton-grass moor

Molinia-nardus moor and
molinia-sedge moor
(wet grass moor)

Practical studies

Oak woodlands are the most complex of all ecosystems in Britain and they give the highest natural productivity possible for any site. Many practical studies of woodlands are possible. Equipment is needed, but simple instruments can be made to carry out quite comprehensive surveys. Each group of five or six people at work on the woodland survey described below used the following equipment.

1. 1 slope measurer—a protractor mounted on a piece of wood (fig 4.c).
2. [1]4 quadrat sticks, 1 metre long, marked off at 0.5 metre (fig 4.d).
3. 4 pieces of string 10 m long wound round a notched piece of hardboard.
4. 4 pieces of string 4 m long (or use the 10 m strings marked 4 m from each end). (Fig 4.e.)
5. [1]1 hypsometer to make direct readings of the height of trees (fig 4.f).
6. 1 surveyor's tape (100 m) (fig 4.g).
7. [1]1 quarter girth tape (a plain tape marked off in units of 3.1 cm, so that when the circumference of the tree is measured, the measurement is automatically divided by 3.1 (π) giving the diameter directly in cm (fig 4.h).
8. 1 lady's spade (fig 4.j).
9. 1 trowel.
10. plastic bags for soil samples.
11. soil labels. (Fig 4.k.)
12. [1]pH kit (cheap home-made kits can be carried in a sawn-off plastic fruit-juice or washing-up-liquid container) (fig 4.l).
13. [1]1 Martin soil colour chart (fig 4.m).
14. Ruler or tape for measuring depth of soil horizons (fig 4.n).
15. [1]Work sheets.

This equipment was used to find the following.

1. The angle of slope of the site.
2. The percentage cover and percentage frequency of plant species. Nested quadrats of 0.5 × 0.5 m, 1 m × 1 m, 4 m × 4 m, and 10 m × 10 m were used for the moss, herb, shrub and tree layers, respectively. A shrub is defined as being under 3 m in height. A tree is over 3 m and has a single trunk and a well-defined crown.
3. The height and diameter of each

[1]Detailed instructions for making these are given in: Rona Mottershead, 'Practical Biogeography', *Teaching Geography*, no. 23, *Geographical Association*, Sheffield, 1974

tree in the quadrat. The diameter is measured at 1.3 m above the ground. The quarter girth tape automatically converts the circumference measurement into the diameter. The hypsometer gives a direct reading of the height and saves much tedious calculation.

4. The nature of the soil profile. A small pit two spade widths square was dug. Horizon depths were recorded and tests of soil colour, texture and pH were made for each horizon. (See pp. 37–46 for detailed work on soil.)

Fig 4.c
Slope measurer

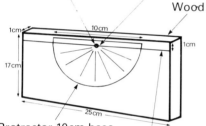

Put washer between protractor and wood to allow protractor to swing freely. Screw through centre of protractor.

Wood

1cm

10cm

17cm

1cm

25cm

Protractor 10cm base. Base line of protractor is placed centrally on black line.

Draw in black line 1cm down and parallel to top edge of wood.

Sight up or down slope. Surveyor's partner reads the angle.

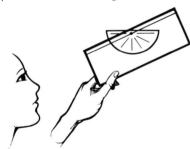

Fig 4.d
4 metre quadrat sticks

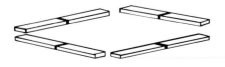

Fig 4.e
10m string

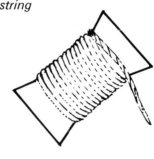

Fig 4.f
Hypsometer

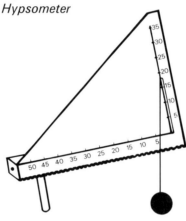

Fig 4.g
Surveyor's tape

Fig 4.h
Quarter girth tape

Fig 4.j Lady's spade

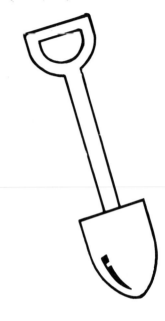

Fig 4.k
Trowel, plastic bag, labels

Fig 4.m
Martin colour chart

8 Grey
7 Red
6 Orange
5 Yellow
4 Lt. Brown
3 Mid Brown
2 Dark Brown
1 Dark Grey

Fig 4.n
Ruler

Fig 4.1

Container is 4.5-litre orange-juice plastic container (or similar) with edge and pourer cut out about 65 mm in from each corner

Bottles are plastic, 75–100 mm high. Containing:
white powder – one with plastic screw top; dark liquid – one with dropper nozzle in screw filter cap; water – one with dropper arm in screw cap.

Spatula, black plastic, flat

Tube stand is wood. One piece about 30 mm square x 160 mm long with six 16 mm holes, glued to other piece about 75 mm x 12.5 mm x 160 mm long.

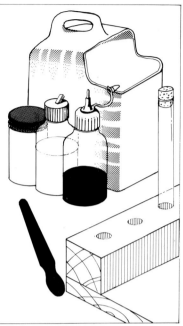

Newgate Wood, Yorkshire: a field study

Site features

Date: June 1977
Grid ref: 874927
Height: 230 m above MSL
Angle of slope: 21°
Aspect: north-east facing
Position on slope: half way up
Parent material: lower calcareous grit (a limy sandstone in the oolitic series)

Table 4.p

Vegetation survey

	% cover	% frequency	Av height	Av diameter	Av number per 100 m²
Tree layer (10 m × 10 m quadrat)					
Sessile oak	80 (canopy)	100	14 m	25 cm	8
Shrub layer (4 m × 4 m quadrat)					
Bramble	—	10	1.5 m		
Rose	—	10	1.5 m		
Rowan	—	10	2.8 m		
Herb layer (1 m × 1 m quadrat)					
Nardus grass	10	100	25 cm		
Fern bracken	20	100	60 cm		
Other grasses	10	80	30 cm		
Wood anemones	6	20	15 cm		
Wild garlic	5	20	6 cm		
Dog's mercury	9	30	20 cm		
Bluebells	4	50	15 cm		
Primroses	3	40	10 cm		
Tormentil	3	40	5 cm		
Bar ground	30	—	—		
Ground layer (0.5 m × 0.5 m quadrat)					
Mosses	20	100	2 cm		

Vegetation Survey

exercises

BIOMASS

It is possible to calculate the biomass of the tree trunks in this particular woodland and eventually to estimate the total biomass per square metre of the woodland as a whole and its rate of productivity. The volume of the trunk of a tree is taken to be half the volume of a cylinder of the tree's height and diameter at 1.3 m above ground. The reduction by a half allows for trunk tapering.

Vol in cu cm $= 0.5 (r^2 \times \pi \times ht)$

$$\frac{(0.5 \text{ diam in cm at } 1.3 \text{ m above ground})^2}{2} \times 3.1 \times ht \text{ (in cm)}$$

Remember to express all measurements in cm.
Calculate the following.

4.4 The average biomass of the trunk of an oak tree.

4.5 The biomass of all the oak-tree trunks in 100 square metres.

4.6 The biomass of the trunks per square metre.

4.7 To get a rough indication of the volume of biomass per square metre in the roots, branches and leaves as well as in the trunks, multiply your answer to 4.3 by 1.5. This biomass proportion— 2:1 trunk: roots, branches and leaves—is only approximate, as great variations can occur with age and species of tree.

4.8 The dry weight of oak is 0.57 gm/cc. Calculate the dry weight of the biomass in gm/m^2.

4.9 These trees are about 40 years old. What is the average productivity per m^2 per year?

4.10 Normally in oak woodland 85% of the biomass is in the trees. To estimate the total biomass of all living plants in this oak woodland, multiply your answer to 4.5 by 1.176. This figure then includes shrub, grass, moss, etc, biomass as well as the tree biomass.

PRODUCTIVITY AND INPUTS

The productivity of oak woodland on this site is rather low. To try to account for this we need to consider the inputs of energy, nutrients and water, and the site and climatic conditions. The meteorological office and the local water board supplied climatic data. *The Institution of Heating Ventilating Engineers Guide*[1] gives figures for calculating energy inputs.

[1]Curwen Press, 1970

exercises

ENERGY INPUTS (fig 4.q)

4.11 Draw a bar chart of monthly amounts of the maximum possible energy coming in from the sun.

4.12 Shade in the top third of each column in black. This is the probable energy lost due to cloudiness, air pollution and the unfavourable aspect here.

4.13 Shade in blue those columns whose monthly mean temperatures fall below 5.6°C. These are the cold months when most plants cannot use available energy for photosynthesis.

4.14 The unshaded area of the columns now represents the total amount of energy available per year for photosynthesis. This amount may be either estimated from your bar chart or calculated from the monthly figures.

4.15 Try to find approximately how much energy per square centimetre of floor area is used in your local factory and estimate % energy loss. Compare this efficiency (100 − % loss) with the photosynthetic efficiency of plants, which is about 1%.

4.16 Look at the aspect of the oak

Table 4.q. Climatic data

Table 4.q. Climatic data

Maximum possible monthly amounts of energy coming in from the sun at 55°N (kilocalories/cm²)

J	F	M	A	M	J	Jy	A	S	O	N	D	Total
2.2	4.9	9.9	15.1	20.1	21.0	20.1	15.6	9.6	5.4	2.2	1.6	127.7

Temperatures at 200 metres above MSL (0°C)

J	F	M	A	M	J	Jy	A	S	O	N	D	Av
1.2	1.3	3.4	5.9	9.1	12.1	13.5	13.3	11.4	8.7	3.8	1.8	7.1

Rainfall at Newtondale (mm)

J	F	M	A	M	J	Jy	A	S	O	N	D	Total
90	70	56	59	66	65	74	97	76	78	107	87	928

Estimated potential evapotranspiration (mm)

J	F	M	A	M	J	Jy	A	S	O	N	D	Total
2.3	5.8	18.9	35.8	57.2	66.0	57.5	51.4	25.0	10.7	4.7	1.6	336.9

Number of days of:
Rain (⩾ 0.2 mm)

J	F	M	A	M	J	Jy	A	S	O	N	D	Total
18.2	16.3	16.5	16.3	16.5	13.8	12.6	14.4	13.0	13.2	21.0	19.3	191.1

Snow

6.1	8.3	5.6	2.5	0.2	—	—	—	—	0.2	3.5	4.3	30.7

Snow lying (at 0900 hours)

8.4	7.9	2.7	0.5	—	—	—	—	—	—	2.8	5.8	28.1

Air frost

15.0	14.3	10.8	5.3	1.8	0.1	—	—	0.4	1.7	10.5	15.5	75.4

Ground frost

19.7	19.2	17.0	10.7	5.3	1.4	0.2	0.4	2.6	7.3	16.0	19.3	119.1

Fog (0900 hours)

3.3	0.9	0.8	0.1	0.1	0.1	0.0	0.0	0.7	2.3	2.1	2.6	13.0

Wind—figures not available
(Strong easterly winds blow off the sea)

woodland site. How do you think this will affect energy inputs? Draw a diagram to explain your answer.

4.17 Which aspect would you expect to have the best energy intakes?

4.18 How does aspect affect
(i) the timing of daily inputs?
(ii) the timing of monthly inputs?

4.19 Test the hypothesis that there is no relationship between aspect and vegetative cover. Try to find two steep slopes clothed in semi-natural vegetation with very different aspects—for instance two sides of a river valley. Find their orientation by means of a compass. Make detailed observations of the vegetative cover on a line of transect from one side of the valley to the other. During a sunny day in June, make simultaneous recordings of light intensities at various points along the line of your transect at pre-arranged times. Light meters and synchronized watches will be needed. What other factors besides light could affect the vegetation in your study?

WATER INPUTS

4.20 Using the precipitation figures in table 4.q, draw a bar chart showing precipitation received each month.

4.21 Shade in black at the top of each column the amount which could be lost by evapotranspiration.

4.22 In which months is there a water deficit?

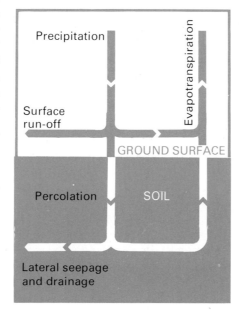

Fig 4.r

4.23 Look at fig 4.r and name three other ways in which precipitation is lost to the ecosystem. Suggest conditions which favour these losses.

4.24 It has been estimated that only 0.1% of the total annual precipitation is incorporated in new organic matter. What amount would be incorporated in 1 square metre of this oak woodland?

4.25 Suggest the effect of the 20° slope on the drainage of this woodland.

4.26 Which part of the slope will be most favourable for tree growth in terms of water input?

4.27 Test the effect of slope on water drainage in the field.

4.28 Test the effect of slope on vegetative growth by observing a slope covered in bracken. Choose a summer month when the bracken is full grown and not dying. On a transect up or down the slope, measure the height of the bracken with a steel tape or tape measure every 15 or 20 metres. Draw a graph of your findings and comment on it. Compare bracken growth on slopes of different angles and aspects in the same area.

NUTRIENT INPUTS

Most nutrients reach plants via the soil. They enter the soil in various ways.
  (i) In precipitation.
  (ii) From plants either
    (a) as nutrients washed in from plant surfaces or
    (b) as litter.
  (iii) From rock weathering.

Table 4.s Movement of nutrients into the soil in oak woodland

	Nitrogen	Phosphorus	Potassium	Calcium	Magnesium	Sodium	Carbon
Percentage in the precipitation above the canopy	19.1	12.3	7.7	17.8	35.0	61.8	2.4
% added to the precipitation by washing from plant surfaces	−1.4	25.1	65.1	24.1	35.8	35.3	8.0
% in litter fall of dead leaves and branches	82.3	62.2	27.2	58.1	29.3	2.9	89.6
Total weight of element added to the soil, gm/m²/yr	4.99	0.35	3.86	4.10	1.32	5.72	219

exercises

Look at table 4.s and answer the following questions.

4.29 Which nutrients reach the soil mainly
  (i) in precipitation;
  (ii) by washing from surfaces?

4.30 Which four nutrients reach the soil mainly in the litter?

4.31 How, other than from plants, do
  (i) calcium and
  (ii) nitrogen reach the soil?

4.32 Apart from uptake by plants, how may nutrients be removed from the soil? Which nutrients are lost mainly in this way?

Dynamics of a woodland ecosystem

4.33 Draw a sketch of fig 4.t and enter in the boxes the quantities you have calculated so far (calories, cu cm, gm/m²/yr as appropriate). The inputs from rock weathering are more difficult to measure. The soil system is dealt with more fully on pp. 37–46.
  What are the main limitations to productivity in the oak woodland?

The plant community

The oak trees, brambles, grasses, bracken and mosses in Newgate Wood are all competing with each other for light, nutrients and water. They are able to survive because they occupy different layers or strata of the environment (see fig 4.u).

The plants in this oak woodland are not necessarily the only plants that could grow there: this environment could probably meet the requirements of many other plants. The species present are those that reached the site

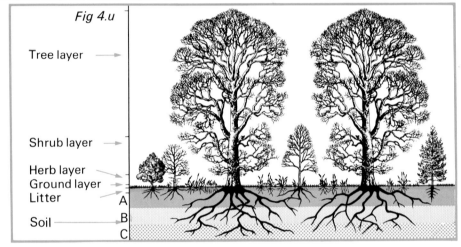

Fig 4.u

Tree layer →

Shrub layer →

Herb layer →
Ground layer →
Litter   A
Soil   B
    C

first and established themselves well enough to resist competition. They grow together because, like Jack Spratt and his wife, they have slightly different requirements or life cycles and can make slightly different uses of the soil and atmosphere. For instance wood anemones flower before the trees start to leaf, wild garlic flowers while the leaves are bursting on the trees and dog's mercury is shade-tolerant. STRATIFICATION of vegetation, both above and below ground, also allows different plants to occupy slightly different micro-habitats or niches, and so survive. Plant groups which grow together in this way have certain compositions and structures which result from interactions between the plants and between the plants and their environment. Such a group of plants is called a PLANT COMMUNITY.

DOMINANCE

Usually in an oak woodland 85% of the biomass is in the trees and only 15% in the other three layers of vegetation. The plants which contain the largest percentage of the biomass are called the DOMINANT plants. They are usually the tallest and the largest. They have the greatest influence on the environment, they contribute most of the litter to the soil and they take most from the soil. They create their own MICROCLIMATE, by modifying temperature, light and humidity and by casting shade.

exercises

4.34 In the field, use a thermometer and light meter to compare the temperatures and light conditions simultaneously at the edge and in the heart of a wood. Compare the percentage cover of plants in the ground and herb layers of the two areas.

4.35 Compare two woods with different types of trees by carrying out surveys similar to that described in this chapter.

4.36 Write a page on: 'oak woodland gives the highest possible natural productivity in Britain'.

ZONES AND ECOTONES

The oak woodland ecosystem de-

Fig 4.t

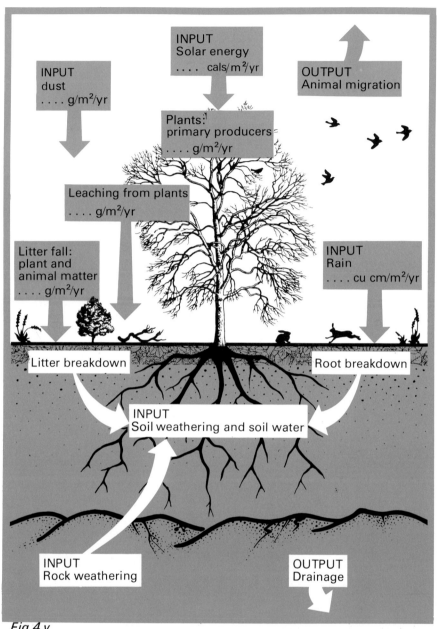

Fig 4.v

scribed on page 32 is unique to its own particular site. Another site with very different physical and biotic conditions will have a very different community. Thus a pattern of communities has evolved over the earth's surface (see fig 8.a). The patches of which the pattern is formed can be considered on scales varying from a tiny rock ledge to a whole tropical rain-forest. Except where man has intervened, there are usually no sharp lines delimiting one zone from the next; except perhaps at a very sharp change in the angle of slope, or between a water and a land surface. Rather there is a continuous gradation between them. The transitional zone is called an ECOTONE, and can vary greatly in scale. It has a greater number of species than do the zones on either side. The plants of one environment grade into those of the next in response to the environmental gradient. The more gentle the gradient, the wider the zone. You can find these zones of transition by counting the species along a line of transect (say from a valley bottom up a slope to a hill top).

Man has created sharp boundaries between plant communities: for example, at field boundaries between different crops, or between farmland and unreclaimed land.

Man chooses to live on the forest edge. Wherever he settles he tends to maintain forest-edge communities. In the past he created clearings in the forest and he has now reduced many former forests to scattered patches of wood interspersed with grassland and cropland. If he settled on former treeless plains, he planted patches of trees to create a similar pattern. Even in towns today he plants trees in his garden. Why do you think he behaves like this? How would you define a forest edge in ecotone terms?

Food webs
Fig 4.v shows a food web based on an oak woodland.

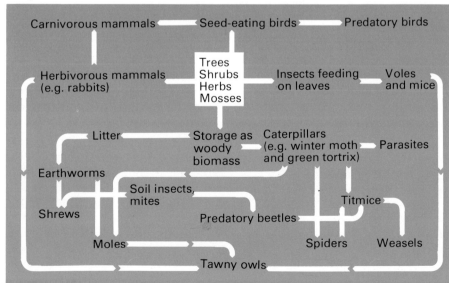

exercises

4.37 At what trophic levels are (i) the titmouse; (ii) the tawny owl found?

4.38 What would happen to the sys-

Fig 4.x

tem if there was (i) a plague of insects feeding on leaves? (ii) a sudden increase in predatory beetles?

Animal biomass in this ecosystem is very small in relation to that of the plants. As you can see from the food web, there is a great diversity of fauna, and usually a greater variety of animals lives in the soil than on or above it.

4.39 Why do you think this occurs?

4.40 Choose a piece of woodland and make a survey similar to the one described in this chapter. The densities of various woods are given in table 4.w.

4.41 Coniferous plantations are the easiest to survey, as their trees have single, straight trunks and the dates of planting are often available from the Forestry Commission. Choose two areas of woodland with trees of the same type but different ages, e.g. 30 years and 60 years. Compare the two in terms of
(i) number of trees per 100 square metres;
(ii) rates of productivity;
(iii) ground and herb layer vegetation;
(iv) light conditions.

4.42 Choose two areas of woodland of different type but similar site conditions and similar ages. Compare their productivity.

4.43 Choose two areas of woodland of the same type and age but very different site conditions, e.g. drainage or aspect, and compare them.

4.44 A food web based on pine trees is given in fig 4.x. What would happen if there were a sudden increase in the number of rabbits?

4.45 In order to be able to feed at all, rabbits gnaw to wear down their teeth, which grow continuously; in this way they inflict much damage on young trees. Plants unpalatable to rabbits include bracken, elder, bramble, broom, ground ivy, wood sage, ragwort, forget-me-nots, wild mignonette, rock roses, stonecrop, night-shade, hemlock, thistles and

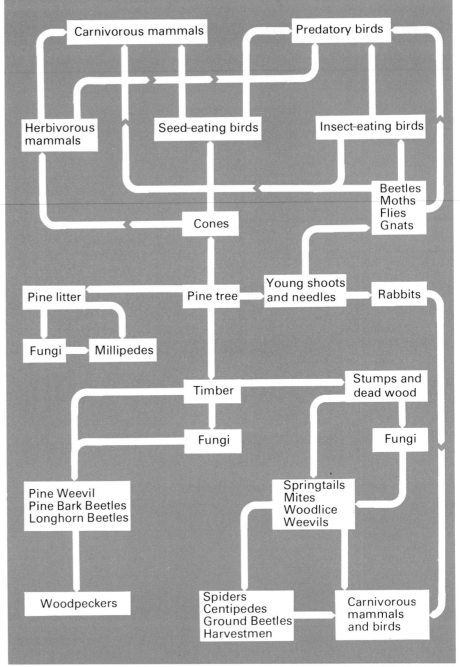

stinging nettle. Try to find a patch of land protected by a rabbit-proof fence and compare the vegetation inside and outside.

4.46 Make a study of the effects of rabbits in a Forestry Commission area.

4.47 Devise work in the field to test the following hypotheses.
(i) There is no relationship between slope and semi-natural vegetation.
(ii) There is no relationship between soils and semi-natural vegetation.
(iii) There is no relationship

between geology and semi-natural vegetation.

Table 4.w

Average figures of specific weights for converting volume (cu cm) of fresh timber into weights (gm) of dry wood.

Norway spruce	0.39	Beech	0.56
Silver fir	0.37	Oak	0.57
Scots pine	0.42	Ash	0.57
European larch	0.47	Maple	0.54
Douglas fir	0.42	Elm	0.46
Weymouth pine	0.32	Birch	0.51
		Alder	0.43

These figures may vary up to 10% either side of the mean.

5 The soil

Fig 5.a is a sketch of the soil profile of Newgate oak wood, shown in fig 5.b. Four HORIZONS or layers were observed and sketched in the field. For each horizon, the depth, colour, texture, pH, water conditions, stoniness and position were recorded and letters ascribed according to the table of soil horizon categories on p. 41.

To explain the characteristics of soil we need to understand the processes at work. Read the account below and answer the following questions on the oak woodland soil. Most explanations involve more than one reason.

exercises

5.1 Why is it a shallow soil? *- Slope steep*

5.2 Why is it sandy?

5.3 Why does the pH vary in each horizon?

5.4 Why is the A horizon dark brown and the B horizon light brown?

5.5 Why is the B horizon stony?

5.6 Why is there a good crumb structure in the A horizon?

5.7 Why is there a litter layer?

5.8 What is the annual precipitation here (table 4.q) and why is the soil well drained?

5.9 Where does this soil system get its energy?

5.10 What are the main processes which formed this soil?

5.11 If ice removed the original soil from this part of Britain in the last ice age, what is the maximum age of the present soil?

5.12 What major group of British soils does this example belong to? Justify your answer. *Brown Earths*

Fig 5.a

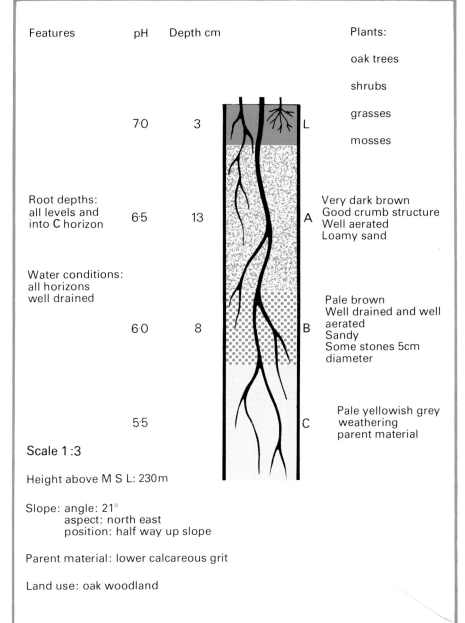

Features	pH	Depth cm		Plants:
				oak trees
				shrubs
	7·0	3	L	grasses
				mosses
Root depths: all levels and into C horizon	6·5	13	A	Very dark brown Good crumb structure Well aerated Loamy sand
Water conditions: all horizons well drained	6·0	8	B	Pale brown Well drained and well aerated Sandy Some stones 5cm diameter
	5·5		C	Pale yellowish grey weathering parent material

Scale 1 :3

Height above M S L: 230m

Slope: angle: 21°
      aspect: north east
      position: half way up slope

Parent material: lower calcareous grit

Land use: oak woodland

Fig 5.b

Dynamics of the soil ecosystem

Soil is a residual layer of material which has accumulated over a long period and in which plants grow. It can be regarded as an ecosystem and has the major components of abiotic substances, consumers and decomposers (see fig 1.u). Producers, however, are relatively insignificant, algae being the only photosynthetic organisms present. For its energy, the soil depends mainly on the residues of plants and animals from outside the system. The great variety of animals living in the soil (fig 5.c) are fed by detritus. As with all ecosystems, the functioning of the soil depends upon inputs and outputs.

Inputs from parent material
PARENT MATERIAL which underlies the soil contributes abiotic substances. The term parent material includes soft substances, such as boulder clay and alluvium, as well as hard rocks like sandstones, limestones, and granite. Ninety-nine per cent of the earth's crust consists of only eight elements; these do not occur independently but are always combined in various ways to form rocks of varying character.

Table 5.d

Oxygen (O)	46.7	%
Silicon (Si)	27.7	
Aluminium	8.07	
Iron (Fe)	5.05	
Calcium (Ca)	3.65	
Sodium (NA)	2.75	
Potassium (K)	2.58	
Magnesium (Mg)	2.08	

There are also small quantities of titanium (Ti), hydrogen (H), phosphorus (P), manganese (Mn), sulphur (S), and carbon (C, in fossil fuels).

The parent material is broken down by the physical processes of heating and cooling, which cause expansion and contraction, by frost shattering, by alternate wetting and drying; and by the action of roots and burrowing animals. Slightly acid rain also causes chemical weathering (fig. 5.e).

Sometimes, during the chemical breakdown of rocks, rainwater absorbs so much basic material that its pH rises above 6.7; it is then incapable of any further reaction and this type of rock weathering ceases. This partly accounts for the shallow soils formed in limestone areas.

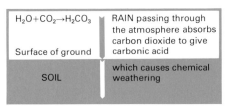

Fig 5.e

Fig 5.f

The crystals are split by physical weathering. The feldspars and micas undergo chemical change to form clay minerals.

$H_2O + CO_2 + KAl\,Si_3O_8 \rightarrow$
(water) (carbon dioxide) (feldspar, alumino silicate of potash)
$Al_2Si_2O_5(OH)$ a clay mineral
$+ Si\,O\,(Olt)_2$ silicic acid
$+ K_2CO_3$ potassium carbonate, removed in solution

The weathering of granite is explained in fig 5.f. The soil particles formed by physical and chemical weathering are classified according to size.

Table 5.g

Particle size	Grade size
2 to 0.05 mm diameter	sand
0.05 to 0.002 mm diameter	silt
less than 0.002 mm diameter	clay

If HUMUS is formed from the breakdown of plant and animal residues, the soil particles are coated with a black, amorphous, jelly-like substance.

Soil particle   Black coating of humus

If the parent material, such as sandstone, contains a high proportion of quartz, it will break down physically almost entirely into sand-sized particles which will remain chemically inert and give a sandy soil. If the parent material, such as granite, is broken down chemically as well as physically, the resultant soil will contain a proportion of clay-, silt- and sand-sized particles.

Soil texture
A soil having fairly equal proportions of sand, silt and clay is called a LOAM. A soil having more than about 30% by weight of clay-sized particles is described as clayey. (Fig 5.h.) In the field a five-fold classification of soil can be made by rolling the wetted soil in the hand and forming shapes progressively: wet the soil and squeeze until no more water comes out, work it in the hands for a minute, then make the various shapes in the order given, starting with a cone. The finale shape achieved denotes the texture. (Table 5.j.)

Fig 5.h

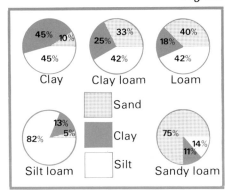

Table 5.j Soil texture

Shape	Classification
1. cone	sand
2. ball	loamy sand
3. worm or roll	loam
4. bent worm which cracks	clayey loam or loamy clay
5. smooth bent worm	clay

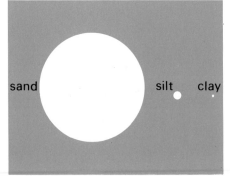

Fig 5.c

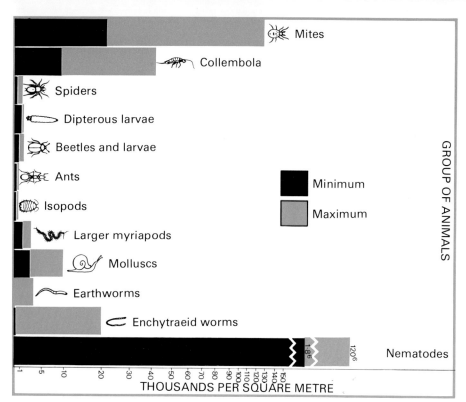

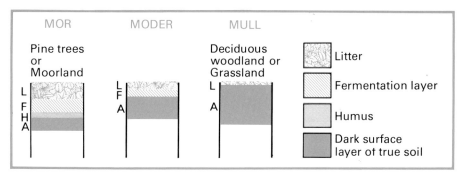

Fig 5.l

Thus if all five shapes can be made, the soil is a clay; if the third but not the fourth shape can be made, it is a loam. Water drains more quickly through sand-sized particles than through clay. Clay minerals are chemically active. They also have COLLOIDAL properties which occur with particles between 0.005 microns and 0.2 microns in diameter, usually dispersed evenly throughout another material: for example milk, which consists of globules of fat dispersed in water. When the particles come together, or FLOCCULATE, spaces are left between the larger groups of particles. (Fig 5.k.)

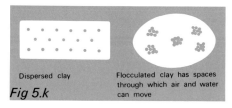

Dispersed clay

Flocculated clay has spaces through which air and water can move

Fig 5.k

The farmer causes clay particles to flocculate by adding lime and manure and so improves the soil's aeration and drainage.

Inputs from organic sources
The movement of nutrients into the soil by washing from plant surfaces and by litter fall was indicated in table 4.s. Litter may range from slightly alkaline to acid, according to the nature of the plant material. For instance beech leaves are rich in bases and pine needles are very acid. Acid conditions develop in soils under coniferous forests and heaths, and these inhibit the activity of the consumers—such as earthworms—and the decomposers—such as bacteria—so that breakdown of plant material is slow. In pinewoods and moorlands, litter accumulates on the surface, a FERMENTATION LAYER of partly broken-down material occurs beneath the litter and further down still a thin layer of humus develops. This surface structure is called MOR. In areas such as deciduous woodland and grassland, where litter is slightly more alkaline and the soil well drained and areated, earthworms and bacteria thrive and organic matter is broken down and incorporated into the soil each year. A deep litter layer does not accumulate here, except temporarily when leaves fall in autumn, or if local

climatic conditions inhibit bacterial activity. The incorporated humus which develops under more alkaline conditions is known as MULL. The form of organic matter intermediate between mor and mull is known as MODER. (Fig. 5.l.)

In waterlogged and anaerobic (airless) conditions, the organisms of decay are inhibited; normal (aerobic) decomposition is arrested; and peat accumulates. Decomposition takes place when man drains the peat to admit air. Such peat soils are very rich indeed because of the accumulation of humic material, especially if the plants forming the peat originally contained high proportions of bases—as in the alkaline fen peat; acid peats when drained are less fertile. Humus is colloidal and holds even more water than does clay; it can take up to eight or nine times its own volume of water.

INPUTS FROM BACTERIA AND BLUE-GREEN ALGAE
Two extremely important means by

which nutrients enter the soil are by nitrogen-fixing bacteria and by blue-green algae living in the soil. Both fix nitrogen directly from the air and so make it available to plants in the soil. Their significance cannot be over-emphasized. Nitrogen-fixing bacteria process something like fifty-four million tonnes of nitrogen per year for the earth as a whole. (There are also denitrifying bacteria processing comparable amounts—see the nitrogen cycle, fig 1.v).

The significance of nitrogen-fixing bacteria has been known for some time, but recent research has shown the importance of blue-green algae. It has been calculated that in paddy fields these algae fix fifteen to fifty kilograms of nitrogen per hectare during a six-week rainy spell. Blue-green algae are also important as primary colonizers in deserts. In New South Wales, for instance, they fix three kilograms of nitrogen per hectare per year—a very significant amount for a harsh environment

Soil structure

Soil is derived from the breakdown of both parent material and organic matter. Soil particles cling together, aggregate, to form blocks or PEDS. The cement holding them together consists of colloidal, glue-like substances, several of which exist in the soil—black humus, red or yellow ferric hydroxide, or white aluminium hydroxide. The peds which form are of different shapes and sizes. Five shapes are recognized, and these may be further classified according to size (table 5.m).

Good garden soil if crushed in the hand will break down into medium-sized CRUMBS, which will not break down any further. This medium crumb structure is what farmers and gardeners hope to achieve, for it is the best for plants to grow in: water can percolate easily through the tiny passages in this soil, as the finest particles, which could hinder drainage, are held in the crumb. Furthermore air can circulate in the spaces between the particles as well as inside the crumb, and many microscopic soil animals live in the spaces between the crumbs. Seeds germinate more easily in a soil which breaks down into crumbs rather than into larger columns and blocks, as their roots can penetrate crumby soils more easily.

Horizon differentiation

Once a mantle of debris from weathered rocks and decayed plants and animals accumulates on the surface, it is further modified by processes within the soil itself. These are mainly brought about by the action of water and cause the development of well-defined layers or horizons within the soil. In Britain the main processes are LEACHING, MECHANICAL ELUVIATION, PODZOLIZATION and GLEYING.

LEACHING (fig 5.n)

Leaching is the removal of soluble minerals, such as compounds of nitrogen (N), calcium (Ca), magnesium (Mg), sodium (Na), and potassium (K), from the surface layers of the soil by the downward movement of slightly acid rainwater. Some of the soluble minerals are reprecipitated lower down in the soil, but most are removed in the water draining into rivers. The upper layers of the soil thus become more acid and impoverished unless lime or fertiliser is added. Three conditions favour leaching:

(i) heavy rainfall;

(ii) a coarse, sandy soil which allows water to percolate freely, carrying the neutralized minerals with it;

(iii) acid humus which increases the acidity of rainwater percolating through the soil.

It is important not to confuse leaching with bleaching. Leaching does *not* produce pale surface layers in the soil.

MECHANICAL ELUVIATION (fig 5.p)

Fine clay particles may be washed from the surface layers by rainwater and deposited lower down. The clay remains chemically unchanged. This process is called mechanical eluviation and results in a coarse surface layer overlying a layer containing finer particles.

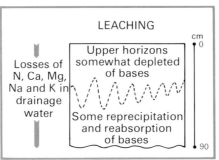

Fig 5.n

Fig 5.p

Table 5.m Soil structure

Type (shape)	Shape of ped	Class (size in mm)				
1. Platy	Thin and horizontal plates	V. thin < 1	Thin 1–2	Medium 2–5	Thick 5–10	V. Thick > 100
2. Prismatic or columnar	Long columns with either flat (prismatic) or rounded (columnar) ends	V. fine < 10	Fine 10–20	Medium 20–50	Coarse 50–100	V. coarse > 100
3. Blocky	Angular or subangular blocks (or polyhedrons	V. fine < 5	Fine 5–10	Medium 10–20	Coarse 20–50	V. coarse > 50
4. Crumby	Small hard granules or crumbs (or spheroids)	V. fine < 1	Fine 1–2	Medium 2–5	—	—
5. Structureless		—	—	—	—	—

PODZOLIZATION (fig 5.q)

This process only takes place when there is a particularly acid mor layer (usually black or dark brown) on the surface. Rainwater percolating through this layer becomes very acid, and capable of breaking down iron and aluminium oxides and washing them out of the surface layers. Iron oxides give a reddish colour to the soil, and their removal leaves the soil bleached white or grey. Podzolized soils thus have a well-defined grey or white layer below the surface.

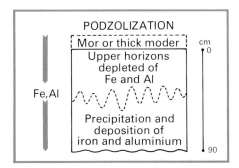

Fig 5.q

The iron and aluminium oxides are redeposited lower down, producing a bright orange or red layer. Sometimes the iron oxide is concentrated in a very thin layer, only one centimetre thick, and forms a hard PAN. This may be so hard that the Forestry Commission, in ploughing moorland, has to use dynamite to break through it. Moreover, this hard pan may be impermeable and cause water to build up in the soil above.

GLEYING

The process by which ferric oxide (Fe_2O_3 or Fe^{III}) is reduced to ferrous oxide (FeO or Fe^{II}) is known as gleying. It occurs in waterlogged anaerobic conditions, and such gleyed soils are a grey or bluish-grey colour. Where gleyed soils are subject to uneven reduction, they are mottled red and grey.

Horizon categories (fig 5.r)

A describes a horizon consisting of well-mixed organic and inorganic material. It is usually near the surface and dark in colour because of the decay of roots *in situ* and the incorporation of litter from above.

B describes a horizon which receives material washed down from above: e.g. bases, fine clay particles or ferric oxides. These are sometimes called illuviated horizons (illuviation means washing in).

C describes the weathered but otherwise little-altered parent material.

Slight differences in A or B horizons are differentiated by number: e.g. A_1 A_2 A_3 etc B_1 B_2 B_3 from the surface down.

E describes a horizon depleted of iron oxides or clay.

Additional letters may be added to A or B horizons to distinguish minor characteristics.

Ah humic staining
Ac horizon from which material has been washed out (eluviated)
Ap ploughed
Au disturbed
Bfe enriched in illuviated iron
Bh humic
Bg gleyed
Bca calcic
Bt clay enriched
Bsa saline

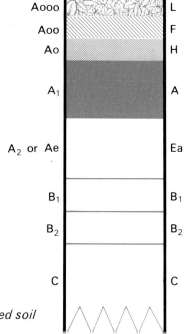

Fig 5.r
The horizons of a podzolized soil with alternative labelling.

Soil patterns

SOIL CLASSIFICATION

The classification of this complex, three-dimensional substance—soil—is very difficult and subject to much controversy. In Britain 1: 50 000 soil maps are based on profile studies in the field. Soil scientists group together similar profiles and then classify the soils according to their common characteristics. Soil profiles are grouped progressively into PEDONS, SOIL PHASES, TYPES and then SERIES (fig 5.t). The soil series are then used as a basis for drawing 1 :50 000 maps, the series being differentiated by local names. The soil series are further combined into sub-groups and groups, which are also mapped at a 1 :50 000 scale (table 5.s).

The soil survey of Great Britain is incomplete and because of its cost is not likely to be completed. Maps and memoirs describing soil properties (1974) are available for the areas shown in fig 5.u.

The classification of soils in Britain is based on the actual characteristics of the soil, such as colour, texture, structure and drainage, which are dependent on local geology, slope and ecological factors. British soil classification must be distinguished from that used on world-scale maps, where soils are zoned according to major regions of climate and vegetation.

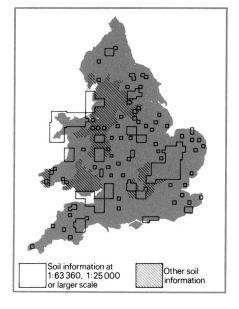

Fig 5.u

41

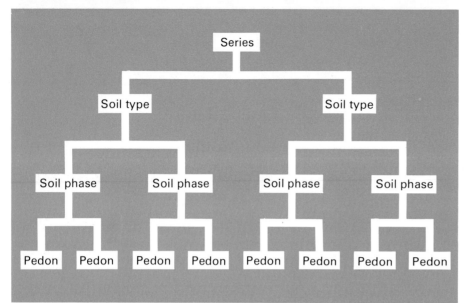

Fig 5.t

Table 5.s *Soil groups and sub-groups in the British Isles*

Major soil groups		Sub-groups	
I	Brown earths	1.	Leached brown earth
		2.	Leached brown earth with gleying
		3.	Acid brown soils
		4.	Acid brown soils with gleying
		5.	Ferritic brown earth
II	Podzols	1.	Podzolized acid brown soils
		2.	Humus iron podzols
		3.	Gley podzols
		4.	Peaty gley podzols
III	Gley	1.	Surface water gley
		2.	Peaty gley
		3.	Ground water gley
IV	Organic	1.	Peat
			(i) Fen peat
			(ii) Raised moss
			(iii) Blanket bog
		2.	Peaty soils e.g. peaty loam
V	Calcareous	1.	Rendzinas
		2.	Brown calcareous soils
		3.	Brown calcareous soils with gleying

On soil maps two other categories are shown

VI Dune sand: sand or a very young soil on unconsolidated material

VII Rock dominant: where the surface is just rock, bare of soil

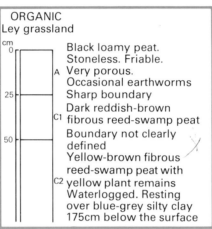

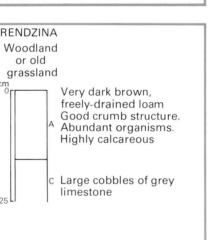

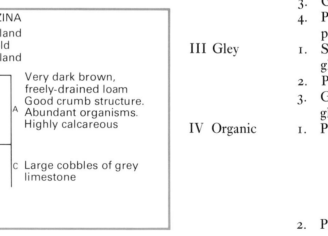

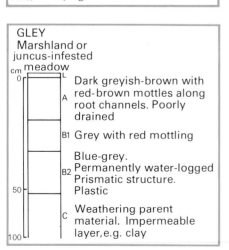

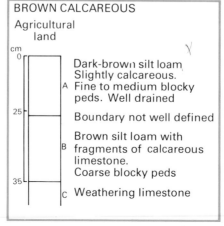

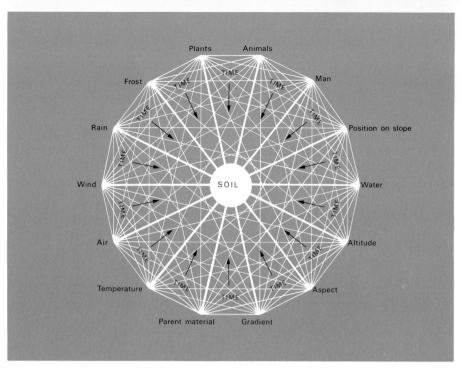

Fig 5.v *The inter-relationship between environmental factors and the soil; and between the factors themselves. The effect of environmental factors increases with time.*

LIMITATION TO THE SOIL ECOSYSTEM AND PATTERNS PRODUCED

A Russian soil scientist, Vasily Do-kuchayev (1846–1903), pointed out that a soil was the result of the interplay of five major factors.
(i) Climate;
(ii) Parent material;
(iii) Organisms—plants and animals;
(iv) Relief and elevation;
(v) Age of the soil.
He considered climate to be the most important and based his classification of world soils on it.

The American soil scientist, H. Jenny, restated this idea in 1941 as:
$s = f(cl,o,r,p,t...)$
cl = external climate
o = all organisms including man
r = major relief form
p = parent material
t = time
$...$ = other possible factors.
The inter-relationships of these five major factors, each of which can be subdivided into further factors, is very complex (fig 5.v).

The influence of two of these factors is described below.

THE INFLUENCE OF PARENT MATERIAL

In young soils the nature of the parent material markedly influences the soil developing on top. Care must be taken, however, in classifying on slopes, as material from a different outcrop of rock may be washed downslope and incorporated in a soil lower down.

The colour of the soil is often influenced by the parent material. Ferric oxide (Fe_2O_3 or Fe^{III}) is orangey-red and gives colour to rocks such as the red sandstones of Devon, and to Devon soils. Another iron oxide, ferrous oxide (FeO or Fe^{II}) is black and imparts a characteristic blue-grey colour to its soil.

Black colour in soils may be due to the presence of manganese. Very often, however, it denotes a high humus content.

Sandstones produce a poor, chemically inactive soil because of their high sand content. A pure sand contains no colloids, is unable to retain in its mass either water or dissolved plant nutrients and is consequently unproductive ('hungry').

Limestone and chalk have thin soils because the carbonic acid rainwater can penetrate only a short distance before its pH rises above 6.7; this is the pH at which weathering of the parent material at the base of the soil ceases. The proportion of acid-insoluble material in limestone is small (less than 1%), which also leads to a thin soil. Soils on chalk or limestone are usually neutral to alkaline, well drained and well aerated. They are not subject to much podzolization or leaching and develop a good stable crumb structure.

In dry climates where the action of water in profile development is at a minimum, and where organic influences are unimportant, soils more closely resemble the underlying rock than they do in wetter regions.

In older soils other factors such as plants and climate have had a longer time to influence the nature of the soil and parent material is less important.

THE INFLUENCE OF SLOPE
(i) Soil movement
Where a slope is over twenty-five degrees, material on the surface is unstable and does not accumulate but moves downslope, leaving bare rock or a discontinuous soil covering.

Where the slope is twenty degrees to twenty-five degrees, there is a slow creeping of the soil downslope, resulting in a thin soil near the top and a thicker soil lower down. This downward movement is often retarded by the roots of plants, so that many slopes have a 'stepped' or terraced ap

pearance; these terraces can be as small as a few centimetres in depth.

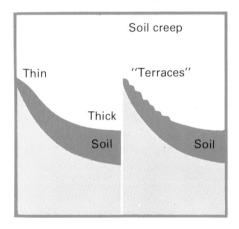

(ii) Soil drainage
Where the slope is over ten degrees, soils are usually well drained; under two degrees they are poorly drained. Fig 5.w shows the variation in drainage down a slope of typical convex-concave shape in the British Isles. The upper, well-drained sites are called SHEDDING SITES; the lower ones RECEIVING SITES as they receive the water draining from above.

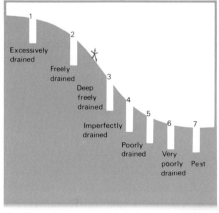

Fig 5.w

(iii) Soil water

The amount of water retained by the soil depends on the relative rates of input to and loss of water from it. Factors affecting these rates include quantity and rate of rainfall, temperature, and soil composition and depth.

There are three types of soil water (fig 5.x).

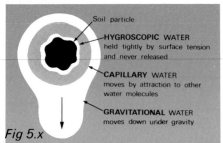

Fig 5.x

When a soil holds as much capillary water as possible, it is said to be at FIELD CAPACITY. In this state there are still pores occupied by air. When it holds as much gravitational water as possible, it is SATURATED and air is excluded. This waterlogging occurs after heavy, continuous rain, where an impermeable layer is close to the surface or where gradients are low.

Clay particles are capable of holding more hygroscopic and capillary water on their surfaces than other sorts of particles. Clay particles can absorb two or three times their own volume of water, which causes them to swell when wet and shrink when dry.

exercises

In the field

5.13 Test the pH of the soil under an oak tree and compare it with that under a coniferous tree close by. Try to ensure that other conditions, such as parent material, slope and precipitation, are similar.

5.14 Test the hypothesis that there is no relationship between soil depth and position on a slope.

In the laboratory

5.15 List possible outputs to oak woodland soil described on p. 37.

5.16 Test the hypothesis that there is no relationship between soil and parent material by means of the following exercise.

MATERIALS REQUIRED

(i) A transparent overlay to cover an area 10 × 10 km on a 1 : 50 000 or 1 : 63 360 map. Draw 100 grid squares with northings and eastings numbered 0 to 10 as in fig 5.y.

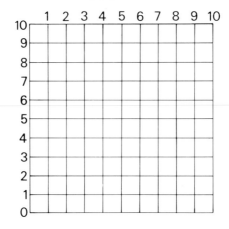

Fig 5.y

(ii) A sheet of random numbers. To produce your own random numbers you need 10 ping-pong balls (or 10 cork balls of 3 cm diameter obtainable from any chemical supplier) and a box. The volume of the box should be about six times that of the balls to give them freedom of movement.

(iii) 1 soil map and 1 drift geology map of the same area, of scale 1 : 63 360 or 1 : 50 000. Suitable areas are on

(a) Sheet 280, the Wells drift and solid combined geology map, and sheet 280, the Wells map of soil survey of England and Wales, between northings 48 and 58 and eastings 40 and 50.

(b) Sheet 83, Formby drift geology, and sheet 83, Formby soil map, between northings 03 and 13 and eastings 29 and 39.

(c) Sheet 75, Preston drift geology, and sheet 75, Preston soil map, between northings 23 and 33 and eastings 40 and 50.

METHOD

Shake the 10 balls in the closed box and remove one at a time; note its number before returning it to the box for reshaking. Repetition of this procedure provides random numbers of any magnitude (i.e. number of digits).

Use 4-figure random numbers as grid numbers to locate points on the overlay placed over the chosen map

areas. Record the random numbers and use the overlay first on the geology, then on the soil sheet. Note the geology and soil type located at each spot defined by the random numbers. Record the major soil group—e.g. brown earth, ground water gley—but *not* the complexes given in the map key.

Count up the number of times a certain soil type occurs on a particular type of geology and record this in matrix form with columns for soil and rows for geology.

Comment on your findings or use the chi-squared test on your results.

5.17 Make a soil survey similar to that for the oak woodland described at the beginning of the chapter. For each horizon describe the depth, colour, pH, texture, water conditions, stoniness, depth of roots and any special features. Record the site features, and land use or vegetation.

Bring enough soil (a few grammes should be enough) back to the laboratory, to make a soil profile using the soil itself as a 'powder paint' to colour the horizons (see Rona Mottershead, 'Practical Biogeography'). Describe and account for the soil's characteristics and give it a group name.

Unravel the causes: an exercise in soil detection

It is very difficult to unravel the interrelating influences on the soil and to decide which particular factor has had the major effect. The three soil profiles in fig 5.z lie at the points marked on a line of transect up a slope on the Yorkshire moors. Try to apply the detective method: accumulate facts, consider possible theories and deduce an explanation of the distribution of these soils.

Facts

exercises

5.18 Draw a cross-section from X to Y with a vertical scale 1 : 1000 and a horizontal scale 1 : 10 000.

5.19 On this cross-section
(i) shade in and name the geological beds, which are nearly horizontal here.

Fig 5.z

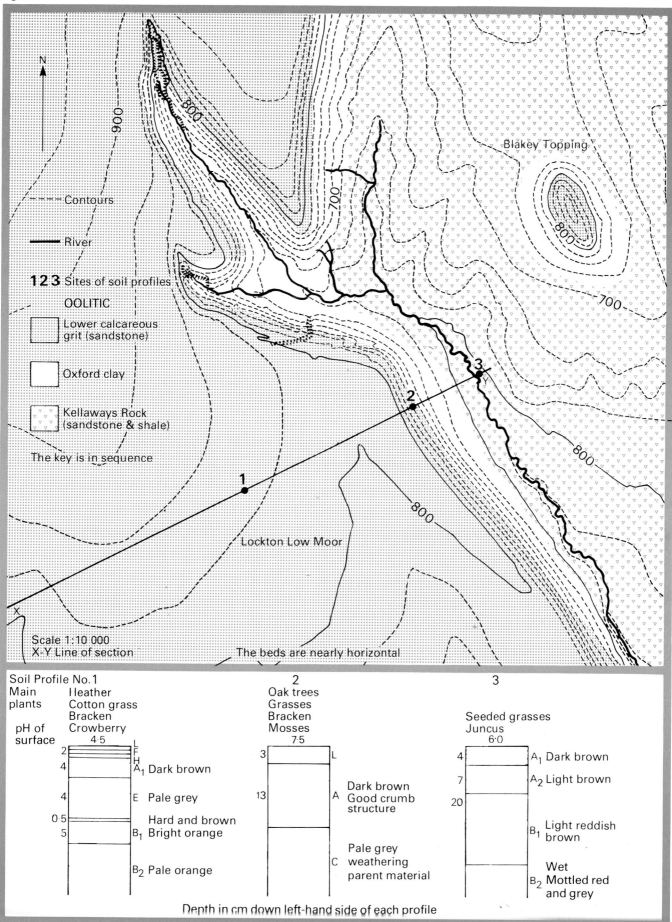

(ii) mark the location of the three soil profiles.

5.20 Give each soil a group name and briefly explain the main process which has produced it.

Theories

(i) ARE THE CAUSES NATURAL?

In 1935 the British soil scientist, G. Milne, put forward the idea that there is a sequence of soil profiles in regular succession down a slope, and that this sequence is due directly or indirectly to topography. He said the nature of a soil is determined by its position on the slope and especially by conditions of drainage. This succession he called a CATENA. An idealized catena is shown in fig 5.aa.

Rarely is such a complete catenary succession found, for such perfectly shaped slopes rarely occur in reality, and parent material often changes down-slope. More complex soils, such as peaty gley podzols, often develop. The British soil scientist, G. R. Clarke, developed the idea of a MIXED CATENA: when different outcrops of rock occur in rapid succession down a major slope, at least two kinds of soil may be found for each outcrop.

Fig 5.aa

(ii) IS MAN THE CAUSE?

In Mesolithic times all three soils probably supported oak woodland. Bronze Age man started to clear the trees on land over 240 metres, first with an axe and then by burning, to maintain heather moorland for grazing his sheep. Over the last hundred years, man has been regularly burning the moorlands every eight to fifteen years to produce young, tender shoots of heather which are more palatable to sheep and grouse. Thus the trees have been unable to regenerate themselves. Continued grazing has impoverished the soil. The custom of burning has caused the continued removal of carbon, nitrogen, sulphur and other elements from the system; although the loss may be only temporary, as there are compensatory mechanisms, such as increased bacterial activity, returning nutrients to the soil. Thus the nutrient store in the soil has decreased; the rates of circulation of nutrients have been reduced; and the acid litter of moorland plants has increased the soil's acidity. Removal of the woodland, too, has increased rates of run-off, erosion and loss of water to streams.

It has been suggested that the podzols of this upland area were once brown earths. This view has been supported by finds, up on the moors, of

brown earth soils preserved beneath Bronze Age burial grounds where soils are normally podzolized.

In moorland valleys, it has been suggested that there has been an increase in soil water following deforestation, resulting in waterlogging and gleying. The steeper slopes in this area have so far retained their woodland, as the gradient is too steep for ploughing and the soil rather thin.

Thus we have two widely differing explanations for the podzols of the upland, the brown earths of the slope and the gleys of the valley.

Deductions

exercises

5.21 Write out Jenny's equation of soil-forming factors (see p. 43). Which two factors are the same for all three sites?

5.22 Of the remaining factors, which one do you suspect causes such wide differences in the soils?

5.23 In the light of the answers to 5.21 and 22 and a consideration of theories (i) and (ii), which do you think has had the greater effect on the distribution of soils—man or nature?

	SHEDDING SITES			RECEIVING SITES	
Relief	Plateau over 300m	Upper slope 175-300m	Lower slope 75-175m	Slope foot 50-75m	Lowland below 50m
Soil	PEAT	PODZOL	SHALLOW BROWN EARTH	GLEY	LOWLAND PEAT
Drainage	Poorly drained	Freely drained	Deep, freely drained	Very poorly drained	Permanent waterlogging
Rainfall	Over 1500mm	1000 to 1500mm	750 to 1000mm	300-750mm	Below 300mm
Man's use of the land	Moorland or afforested	Moorland or afforested	Arable	Meadow	Meadow

6 Substantially changed environments

Lockton low moor

The beautiful purple-clad sweep of the moorlands and the mystery of the ancient oak woodlands we have studied in pp. 28–36 are under attack today, for man is rapidly reshaping the landscape of the North Yorkshire Moors. (Figs 6.a and 6.b.) The farmer is venturing higher up the slopes with his plough and carving out squares of seeded pasture where once the heather thrived; the forester is dynamiting the hard iron pan to plant extensive tracts of sombre, regimented pine trees. The North Yorkshire Moors National Park is trying to guard against too many changes and to regulate their speed and extent; it has rescued small pockets of wild lands to preserve their beauty and to husband as great a variety of plants and animals as possible. The nature reserves managed by the County Naturalists' Trust and sites of scientific interest are shown in fig 6.j.

exercises

6.1 Look at the maps of Lockton Low Moor for 1950 and 1975 (figs 6.c and 6.d), and for each map calculate the percentage cover of the various types of land use by line sampling. To do this you should take in turn each northing numbered 0 to 9 and each easting numbered 0 to 9, and estimate the percentage (to the nearest 1%) of the line which crosses each type of land use. For instance, on the 1950 map, northing 0 crosses 90% moorland, 4% reafforested land and 6% oak woodland. Make sure your percentages add up to 100 in each case. In 1975 the trees on land marked 'moorland with regenerating silver birch, rowan, scots pine' were only tiny saplings, and you should therefore still categorize this land as moorland. To record your findings, set out two tables, one for 1950, the other for 1975. Head the five columns: % cover of (i) moorland, (ii) seeded pasture, (iii) oak woodland, (iv) reafforested land, (v) land not in use. Label the twenty rows northing 0, 1, 2 . . . 9; easting 0, 1, 2 . . . 9. Total each column and find the averages by

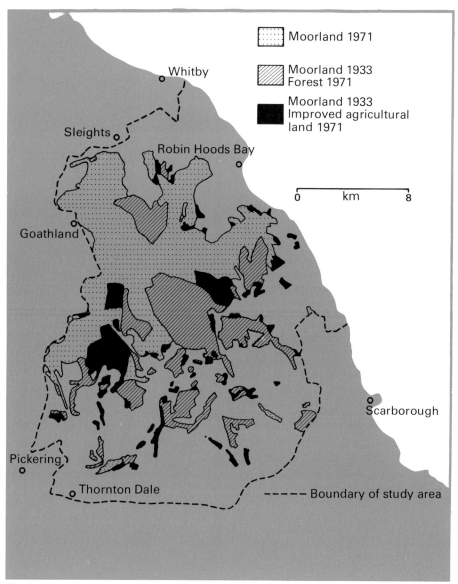

Moorland 1971

Moorland 1933
Forest 1971

Moorland 1933
Improved agricultural land 1971

0   km   8

Whitby

Sleights

Robin Hoods Bay

Goathland

Scarborough

Pickering

Thornton Dale

- - - - - Boundary of study area

Fig 6.a

Fig 6.b

47

dividing by twenty—the number of lines sampled.

6.2 Write a paragraph comparing, in general terms, land use in 1950 with that in 1975.

6.3 Suggest reasons for changes in land use between 1950 and 1975 made by (i) the farmer, (ii) the forestry commission, (iii) the nature-reserve warden.

It is possible to find out the extent of man's impact on the rates of photosynthesis in this area by comparing primary productivity in 1950 with that in 1975. We know from calculations made by scientists that the average net productivities in this environment (at this latitude, at 300 metres above sea level and with approximately 1000 mm precipitation per year) are as follows.

Table 6.e

	dry gm/ m²/yr*	†tonnes ha/yr
heather moorland	600	6
seeded pasture	1600	16
reafforested area	2200	22
oak woodland	1000	10

*N.B. These figures are only approximate and are subject to considerable variation.

† 1 tonne = 1 million gm

1 ha (hectare) = 10 000 m²

exercises

6.4 Calculate the total area of land covered by the map. Give your answer in hectares.

6.5 Using the average land-use figures you have already worked out above, calculate the area (in hectares) of each land-use type in 1950 and 1975.

6.6 You can now calculate the amount of living matter or biomass produced in each land-use area during the years 1950 and 1975 by multiplying the area (ha) by its respective rate of productivity (t/ha/yr). Complete your own copy of table 6.f.

6.7 Which land use remained the same in area in both years and contributed roughly the same amount to the annual production of biomass?

Fig 6.c

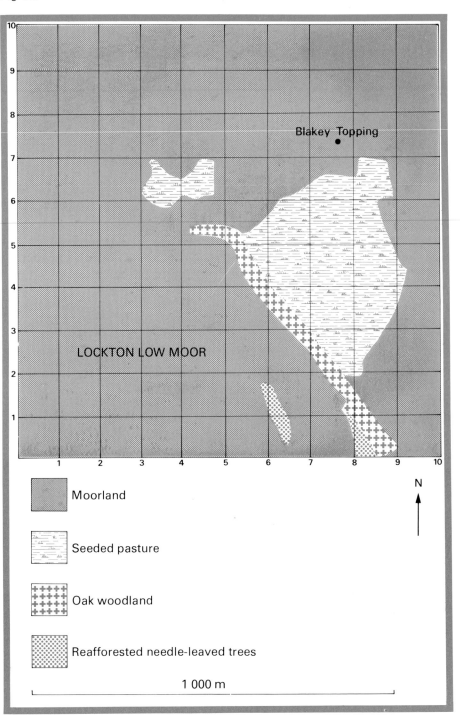

1 000 m

Table 6.f

1950 (or 1975)	% cover	area in ha	rate of prod^y t/ha/yr	biomass produced during the year (in tonnes)
moorland				
seeded pasture				
oak woodland				
reafforested area				
land not in use				

Total biomass produced during the year . . .

Look back to p. 46 and suggest why this land has been left undisturbed.

6.8 In 1975 some land produced no biomass at all. By 1976 what would have happened to this land and by what amount could the biomass of the area shown on the map have been further increased?

6.9 By what proportion has the annual production of biomass changed between 1950 and 1975?

6.10 Which change in land use contributed most to the increased biomass in 1975?

Inputs: by nature and by man

Man can increase primary productivity by using plants which are more efficient producers than others, by increasing the inputs to the ecosystem or by improving environmental conditions. The natural inputs to the area and the environmental conditions have remained roughly the same between 1950 and 1975 (see pp. 32–33); incoming solar energy has remained fairly constant at the rate of 130 kilocals/cm²/yr (maximum on a flat surface), total annual precipitation at 1 125 mm; and the nutrients from the soil and atmosphere have also remained fairly constant, as have climatic conditions such as temperature and wind.

Some plants use these inputs more efficiently and can operate more effectively in these environmental conditions than others.

exercises

6.11 Which of the two semi-natural plant communties shown on fig 6.d is the more efficient? Why do you think this is so?

It is difficult at this stage to say whether pine trees are more efficient than seeded grasses as primary producers, because the farmer and forester have altered the inputs and outputs of the area. That they are more productive than either of the two semi-natural areas of moorland and oak woodland is obvious, but this has only been achieved at great expense. The following extracts from letters from one of the farmers (actually a farming company) operating on Lockton Low Moor and

from the Forestry Commission indicate the nature of the changes they have made and the costs incurred (at 1976 levels).

LETTER FROM G.B. GRANT & SONS (FARMERS) LIMITED, LOUTH, LINCOLNSHIRE TO THE AUTHOR.

'The farm at Newgate Foot, Lockton, has a total acreage of 440 hectares. First reclamation work was begun in 1968 and the total area reclaimed between 1968 and 1970 was 220 hectares.

'Most of the heather received three rotivations before levelling and deep ploughing (30–40 cm). Then followed intensive disc harrowing, and applications of lime and slag (4 tonnes of lime over three years), harrowing, applications of fertiliser N80 P40 K40 (per ha per yr), seeding and rolling. Total cost during the first year of reclamation was about £144 per hectare.

'We originally stocked 800 hill ewes and 10 hill cows, but now we have approximately 800 sheep and 120

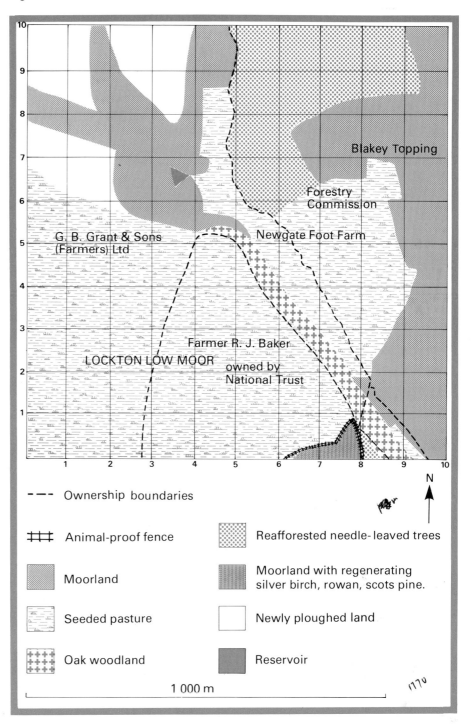

Fig 6.d

Blakey Topping

Forestry Commission

G. B. Grant & Sons (Farmers) Ltd

Newgate Foot Farm

Farmer R. J. Baker

LOCKTON LOW MOOR   owned by National Trust

N

- - - Ownership boundaries

╫ Animal-proof fence

▨ Moorland

▤ Seeded pasture

✚ Oak woodland

▦ Reafforested needle-leaved trees

▥ Moorland with regenerating silver birch, rowan, scots pine.

▢ Newly ploughed land

▧ Reservoir

1 000 m

cattle. The sheep are kept for wool and sale of fat lambs.

'We built the reservoirs between 1969 and 1971 for our own use. We have so far not removed any timber from the steep bank but we shall do so in future. A representative of the company visits the farm daily, travelling from Louth to Lockton by our own aircraft.' (Fig 6.g.)

LETTER FROM THE FORESTRY COMMISSION TO THE AUTHOR.

'The areas planted before 1972 are mainly Corsican Pine (40%) and Sitka Spruce, with some Japanese Larch (10%) on the better soils. Areas planted after 1972 are predominantly Sitka Spruce (85%) with some Japanese Larch (10%) and Lodgepole Pine.

'The new planting to be done in 1976/7 (in the north east corner of your 1975 map) takes over land which was once leased to the Ministry of Defence, but more recently, since 1955, used as a sheep stray.

'Ploughing of the whole area has already begun and it will be planted with predominantly Sitka Spruce (95%), with Japanese Larch and Lodgepole Pine on only a small area. Some hardwoods will be planted on the edge of one small area for amenity purposes. Ploughing costs £35 per hectare and planting costs £52 per hectare. All areas planted up to December 1975 were fertilized in 1971 with Unground Mineral Phosphate Rock. It was spread by helicopter at a rate of 375 kg per hectare at a total cost (including labour etc) of £27.57 per hectare. This gives the plants a good start in life, allowing them to become quickly established and to grow to their full potential. The areas planted with Sitka Spruce had to be sprayed with herbicides against the dominant heather growth, which was depriving the trees of nitrogen and preventing growth. 2.4D (the herbicide) in water was used, at a rate of 400 litres per hectare. In 1976 this cost £18 per hectare. Knapsack sprayers carried on the back were used to do the job.

'A crop of trees is only grown for a certain period of time (or rotation) after which point the mean annual rate of growth begins to drop and the crop is felled. The rotation ages for the tree species here are Sitka Spruce 55 years, Lodgepole Pine 50 years, Japanese Larch 45 years. Depending on the soil conditions, weather etc, individual crops can grow at varying rates, but we calculate that the volume of timber to be obtained from the Blakey Topping area should be on average: Sitka Spruce 543 cubic metres per hectare, Lodgepole Pine 390 cubic metres per hectare and Japanese Larch 450 cubic metres per hectare.'

exercises

6.12 Calculate (in £s per hectare) the total costs to the Forestry Commission of ploughing, planting, fertilizers and herbicides.

6.13 Who paid more—the farming company or the Forestry Commission—in inputs per hectare to produce their crop?

6.14 Describe the nature of the fertilizer added to the soil and comment on the limitations of the natural soil that this fertilizer is designed to overcome.

6.15 Why were herbicides applied by the Forestry Commission?

6.16 Why did the farming company have to plough so deeply? (See p. 45.)

6.17 Comment on the equipment used by the Forestry Commission. What does it indicate about (i) the limitations of the terrain and (ii) the capital investment needed?

6.18 Comment on the capital available to the farming company.

6.19 How long does the Forestry Commission have to wait before a crop is obtained? Are farmers of limited means able to invest capital for so long before getting a return?

6.20 Comment on the scale of the enterprise necessary to produce crops from this environment.

The farming company is growing grass for grazing animals. Approximately ten times as many animals per hectare can be grazed on improved pasture as can be grazed on moorland. However, much of the energy taken in by plants during photosynthesis is lost as it moves up the food chain, only about one tenth being incorporated in the chemical energy of the animal eating vegetation. The scaling down of energy as it moves up the food chain is in the rough proportion of 100 : 10 : 1 at the plant : herbivore : carnivore levels.

exercises

6.21 Calculate the productivity of the ewes in dry gm/m²/yr (the rate of productivity at the second trophic level).

6.22 Which of the two crops—lamb or timber—uses the inputs of nutrients and sun's energy the more efficiently?

6.23 If man (at the third trophic level) were to survive solely on lamb, acting only as a carnivore, what would be the rate of productivity of man (in dry gm/m²/yr).

6.24 What would the productivity of man be if he could live solely on grasses?

6.25 If the population of the earth continued to increase and there

Fig 6.g

was even more pressure on the land to support large numbers of people, what diet might people be forced to adopt?

Unwitting change
The farming company and the Forestry Commission aim to use the earth's resources to produce crops as efficiently as possible. However they may unwittingly trigger off changes which will alter the whole ecosystem and they could even influence ecosystems outside the area of their immediate concern. There are no 'walls' in nature to stop such chain reactions, and in his ignorance of the processes of nature, man has sometimes set in train a series of reactions with catastrophic consequences (see pp. 54–5). Today man is trying to work with understanding of instead of disregard for nature; he is learning to curb his greed for immediate economic wealth and to have more concern for the long-term needs for conservation. However, as we saw in pp. 37–46, man has already altered the nature of the soil on the moors considerably since Bronze Age times and he is continuing to do so. As his technical proficiency improves, so does the scale on which he can effect change: not only in the soil but also in water balances, in micro-climatic conditions and in the numbers and types of animals whose habitats he alters. To discover the kinds of changes man has brought about in the Lockton Low Moor area, allocate the items in the list below which you think apply to (i) Forestry Commission land, (ii) seeded pasture, (iii) the nature reserve. Use all the items—some may apply to more than one category. Then write about a page on the several effects of the farming company, the Forestry Commission or the nature-reserve warden on this part of the moors.

(i) The woodpigeon, long-eared owl, green woodpecker, crossbill and coal tit now inhabit the territory previously occupied by the skylark, wheatear, snipe, golden plover, lapwing and curlew.
(ii) Trampling by holiday-makers is causing erosion of the paths.

(iii) The litter of the man-sown plants added to the soil each year makes it more acid than it would be under semi-natural conditions.
(iv) The soil, stripped of its protective vegetative cover, has been exposed to the erosive effects of wind, rain and snow.
(v) The increased transpiration rates have reduced the run-off of rainwater to streams and could cause increases in rainfall locally.
(vi) The roots of the new plants penetrate deeper than the ones they replace and draw into the ecosystem a nutrient store untapped before.
(vii) This form of monoculture supports a very unstable ecosystem.
(viii) The vegetation has no ground layer.
(ix) Aesthetically the scenery is less pleasing than twenty-five years ago for the subtle mergings of varied colours have given way to single hues and sharp boundaries.
(x) The present vegetation is a better wind-break than the previous plants.
(xi) Eventually, when the trees are fully grown, they could outshade the moorland plants.
(xii) The litter layer on the soil has been reduced, allowing faster evaporation of precipitation and greater compaction of the soil by trampling.
(xiii) The number of plant species is increasing, as the sheep no longer selectively eat out certain palatable plants.
(xiv) The temperatures within the forest are slightly higher than they were within the previous vegetation.
(xv) Colonies of mining bees have been protected and are thriving.

exercises

6.26 The farming company, as suggested in the letter, is hoping to convert the oak woodland to farmland. Suggest as many consequences as you can.

Competing claims and limited land: land use on the North Yorkshire Moors

If we had studied the whole of the North Yorkshire Moors in detail, we would have found many more people all competing to use the land. As our society becomes more complex and more determined to enjoy a higher standard of living, so the number of claimants for land use increases. People still use the land to supply our basic needs for food, materials and minerals; but put increasing demands on the land for leisure activities, water-catchment and waste-disposal. The present day uses of the North Yorkshire Moors are:

Table 6.h
sheep-rearing 6
military purposes 8
water-catchment 7
cattle-rearing 5
grouse-shooting 10
rambling 9
arable farming 4
reafforestation 4
deciduous woodland 11
mineral extraction 3
tips and dumps. 1

exercises

6.27 Rank these uses in order of man's degree of control of the land.
6.28 Draw up a matrix with rows and columns, using table 6.h. Tick those pairs which can co-exist, and put crosses for those pairs which are mutually exclusive.

Class debate on the future of Fylingdales Moor

6.29 Imagine that the class are all concerned with the development of Fylingdales Moor. The area under discussion is bounded on the 1: 50 000 map by eastings 86 and 92 and northings 97 and 04. The vegetation is mainly open moorland with some coniferous woodland and a few tiny patches of oak woodland. A valuable road-building stone called tholeite was once quarried in the Whinstone Ridge. An early-warning system has been built on

Fylingdales Moor, part of which is the property of the Ministry of Defence. The route of the Lyke Wake walk is shown in fig 6.j, this too cutting across this land. There is a nature trail at Falling Foss (in H on fig 6.j), and features of archaeological interest are dotted across the moor. Electricity transmission lines with pylons cross it as well.

Each student, or group, should assume the role of one of the people in table 6.k, and prepare the case for the extension of his own particular work on the moor. Blank assertions that one's own point of view is correct should not sway arguments—facts are needed to prove a point. Each student should prepare the following before the debate.

(i) A sketch map of the area (shown on the 1 : 50 000 map) showing the main features of drainage and relief and the main features of land use relevant to the present discussion.

(ii) A sketch map of his own plan for the future of the area.

(iii) A written report of the plan, supported by graphs, histograms, pie charts, drawings and diagrams (perhaps drawn large enough for display).

Each claimant in turn could make his case, leading to a general debate. Then voting might take place—a suggested format is given in fig 6.l. This debate could occupy several periods or be abbreviated by eliminating some of the claimants. Tables 6.m–s and fig 6.t give information to support students' claims.

Each student should then write an essay from the geographer's point of view, attempting to balance all the arguments as objectively as possible and arriving at a compromise plan. This plan should be flexible enough to cope with future changes.

Table 6.k
The sheep-farmer
The quarry-man
The landowner who rents out his land for grouse shooting
The conservationist
Representatives of
    the Ministry of Defence
    the North Yorkshire Water Authority
    the Forestry Commission
    the local archaeological society
    the North Eastern Electricity Board
    the North Yorkshire Tourist Board
    the Yorkshire Naturalists' Trust
    the Scarborough Council (who for this exercise are *imagined* to be considering using part of the moors for refuse disposal)
    the Lyke Wake Walk Association.

Fig 6.1

Land user	Persuasiveness* 1–5	Should his plan be implemented? Yes/No
Sheep-farmer		
Quarry-man		
etc		

*1–Very persuasive 2–persuasive 3–neutral 4–barely persuasive 5–not at all persuasive

Table 6.m Population

	1933	1955	1970
Billingham	17 972	No figs	34 89(
Guisborough	6 306	8 611	13 93!
Middlesbrough	138 489	147 272	157 18(
Pickering	3 668	4 336	4 45(
Redcar	20 159	27 516	35 62(
Scarborough	41 791	43 985	42 51(
Stockton	67 724	74 155	83 26(
Thornaby	21 233	No figs	28 87(
Whitby	11 441	11 674	12 24(

Table 6.n Human needs
per person per day

For human metabolism	water—2 220 grammes
	food—523 grammes
For sewage disposal	solid 61 grammes
	liquid 2 542 grammes

For washing, disposal of household wastes and sewage, preparation and cooking of food—160 litres of water
For rubbish disposal—448 grammes of rubbish

Table 6.p Recreation

	1949	1972
Average income in GB	£576	£1276
% spent on recreation	2	11
Standard working week	44.8 hours	40.1 hours
	weeks	weeks
Car ownership	2.3 million	12 million

% of workers having paid holiday entitlements of varying lengths	1	1–2	2	2–3	3+	1	1–2	2	2–3	3+
	28	3	66	2	1	—	—	28	5	67

Fig 6.j

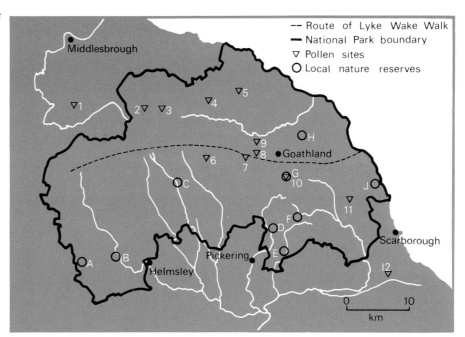

Legend:
-- Route of Lyke Wake Walk
— National Park boundary
▽ Pollen sites
O Local nature reserves

Map labels: Middlesbrough, Goathland, Scarborough, Pickering, Helmsley. Pollen sites 1–12, nature reserves A–J, H, G.

km scale 0 — 10

Fig 6.t

Problems in wake of a walk

By MICHAEL PARKIN

THE Countryside Commission has refused to recognise the Lyke Wake Walk, a 40-mile endurance test across the North York Moors National Park, as an official long distance footpath.

His Mournfulness, the Chief Dirger of the Lyke Wake Club, Mr Bill Cowley, said yesterday that the decision seemed to reflect the typical southern, bureaucratic attitude of people who would not recognise a walk if they saw one.

Mr Cowley founded the Lyke Wake Walk about 20 years ago. His inspiration was an ancient belief that after death the soul has to make a terrible journey across the moors. The Lyke Wake dirge, last heard over a coffin in North Yorkshire in about 1800, reflects this belief:

When thoo frae hence away art passed . . .
To Whinney Mike Moor thoo comes at last
And Christ tak up thy soul.

Mr Cowley set a limit of 24 hours for completing the 40-mile walk. Young walkers tackled the walk in their hundreds and then in their thousands. It became so popular that Mr Cowley formed the Lyke Wake Club, which gave all those who made the arduous crossing a black-edged card of condolence and the rank of dirger. There have now been more than 60,090 crossing of the moor, from Osmotherley in the west to Ravenscar on the coast.

The National Park Committee has "noted with disappointment" the view of the Countryside Commission.

The commission, explaining its decision, said yesterday that it was devoting its resources in this field to improving footpaths for day visitors. The Lyke Wake Walk, at 40 miles, was not long enough to be considered as an official long distance footpath. The shortest footpath recognised, the Dorset Coast path, was 72 miles long. The Lyke Wake also covered some of the same country as a footpath already recognised, the Cleveland Way.

(*Guardian* 26.1.77)

Table 6.s
Crossings of the Lyke Wake Walk

	1st Crossings	Repeat	Total
1955–58	176	15	191
1959	89	23	112
1960	222	33	255
1961	650	150	800
1962	1 100	267	1 367
1963	1 054	409	1 463
1964	1 413	592	2 005
1965	2 042	771	2 813
1966	2 537	723	3 260
1967	3 434	1 059	4 493
1968	4 795	1 235	6 030
1969	4 513	1 286	5 799
1970	5 008	1 166	6 174
1971	5 458	824	6 282
1972	4 546	669	5 215
1973	5 809	467	6 276
1974	6 301	405	6 706
1975	7 812	366	8 178
Total to date	56 959	10 460	67 419

About 6% of crossings are by women.

Here are three further useful references for your work on land use. (i) One-inch maps of the first land utilization survey of Britain, Dudley Stamp, 1933[1]. (ii) 1:25 000 maps of the second land utilization survey of Britain, Alice Coleman, 1960[2]. (iii) Figures of productivity on farmland at Rothamsted where rates are high

Barley   7.5 tonnes per hectare
Beans   3.5
Three-year grass ley   10.9
Potatoes   9.4 (tubers only)
Red clover   6.0
Wheat   12.7

Table 6.q
Imports to Great Britain in 1971

	£s
Meat	465 027
Hides and skins	73 928
Dairy products and eggs	237 768
Cereals	282 776
Feeding stuff for animals	80 756
Manufactured wood	113 921
Manufactured paper	256 703
Wood pulp	161 446
Fertilizers and crude minerals	63 468

Table 6.r

Annual loss of farmland to urban and other uses in England and Wales is 20 243 hectares

Industry uses 75% of all water stored in reservoirs

Imports to Great Britain in 1971

Surfaced roads in Great Britain in 1971—336 852 (including 1 600 km of motorway). There are plans for building 5 635 more km of roads by the 1980s

exercises

6.30 Write an essay justifying the preservation of wilderness in the British Isles, or any other chosen area. Refer to: the wilderness as a resource pool, man's spiritual health, gene pools of wild organisms, ecological research, oxygen and carbon dioxide balances, and man's moral view of his own importance and his right to cause the extinction of other living beings.

[1]Oxford University Press   [2]Stanford

7 Spoiled soils

exercises

7.1 Fig 7.a shows the areas in Lincolnshire affected by soil erosion in 1968. Read the following account and

(i) describe the natural state of the soil;

(ii) list in detail at least eight mistakes that recent farmers have made;

(iii) suggest at least four measures which the farmers could take to prevent such a tragedy recurring.

Farming in Lincolnshire

In recent years agricultural practices have changed considerably. In the eighteenth and nineteenth centuries, small, hedged fields were farmed in rotation: grass, root crops and cereals being grown in soils improved by animal manure.

Today farmers have removed many hedges because of the high value of land and the demands of mechanical cultivation. The percentage of land under grass has decreased and that under cereals has increased. Some farmers grow barley every year. They use only chemical manures and burn the straw and stubble on arable land each year.

The Lincolnshire soils are light, being derived from calcareous and sandy parent material in the uplands, and alluvium and fen peat in the lowlands. The soils are disc-harrowed to a fine seedbed in the spring.

In March 1968 the soils were abnormally dry, having received that year only about half the rainfall normally expected. The number of frosts in February had been significantly higher than usual. The mid-March winds were westerly and strong.

The result was an extremely severe WIND-BLOW of the soils. Many roads were partially blocked, traffic was disrupted and the cost of soil clearance was considerable. Clearing operations in Lindsey cost £4 000. Farmers not only had many of their crops spoilt, but also had to clear ditches and drains, at a cost of £5 per 20 metres. This cost the farmers of the Isle of Axholme £17 500.

The most serious problems were the loss of topsoil and and the decline in fertility associated with it. In Kesteven 6 500 hectares were affected and 2 500 hectares in Lindsey. No figures are available for Holland (Lincolnshire).

Soil degradation can also be induced by industrial activity, as is illustrated by the following exercises.

The Lower Swansea Valley

exercises

7.2 Look at fig 7.b and name three types of soil degradation shown there.

7.3 State, with reasons, which type of soil degradation you consider to be the most serious?

The valley of the River Tawe receives about 1000 millimetres of rain a year and was well wooded until sulphurous fumes killed off all the vegetation in the eighteenth and nineteenth centuries. The prevailing south-westerly winds carried these fumes from the metal industries of the Swansea valley.

The soil was laid bare and open to the forces of erosion. The first stage was on slopes as gentle as three degrees, where the top five centimetres became 'puffy' in appearance and easily removed by surface washing. The second stage was the development of about a hundred gullies, sixty to seventy-five centimetres deep. Other gullies, fed by permanent springs or outside the immediate area, were four to five metres deep. The soil between the gullies, having lost its A and B horizons, looked like a barren stony waste.

exercises

7.4 The weight per hectare of soil fifteen centimetres deep is normally about 500 tonnes. Here, thirty to forty-five centimetres of soil have been removed from 1 250 hectares.

Calculate

(i) the total weight of soil lost;

(ii) the rate of loss, assuming that it took place over about 200 years.

7.5 Severe air pollution has now ceased; and in 1966, after four years of study, the Lower Swansea Valley Project put forward a comprehensive plan to redevelop this area.

What field studies would you have suggested and what recommendations might you have made for improving this area?

Mid-Wales sheep 'burrows'

On the uplands near Plynlimon, in Montgomeryshire, (Powys), sheep burrow into the sides of valleys to find shelter from the wind and rain. They create quarter-moon-shaped scars seventy-five to one hundred centimetres in diameter and thirty to fifty centimetres high, undercut to a depth of twenty to thirty-five centimetres. These 'burrows' obviously do not occur on the flatter tops but on slopes varying between twenty-five degrees and thirty-five degrees, high up on the valley sides. The vegetation in this area varies from bilberry-dominated moorland, with nardus grasses and mosses, to patches of bracken and gorse. Rainfall is heavy, over 1600 millimetres, and falls in frequent, heavy showers or thunderstorms. The soils are podzolic and shallow, about fifteen to twenty-five centimetres deep, overlying shale or mudstones.

Once the burrows have been formed, rapid SHEET EROSION occurs: the whole surface-soil, subsoil and rock fragments, to a depth of sixty-five to one hundred centimetres—slips downslope en masse. All this material is eventually removed in the flood-waters of the valley streams. Rock fragments, slipping downslope, bruise and break up the thin vegetative cover. Once soil movement starts, the eroded areas coalesce sideways. T. M. Thomas' research in 1965, near Machynlleth, showed that 20 out of the total 360 hectares of his study area had been affected by sheet erosion. He forecast that a further 70 hectares could suffer the same loss of soil if unrestricted sheep grazing continued. By comparing the weathering of slate in quarries nearby, for which dates of working were known, with weathering on the scree slopes, he estimated that much of the erosion must have taken place in the last one hundred to one hundred and fifty years.

exercises

7.6 Calculate the volume (in cu cm)

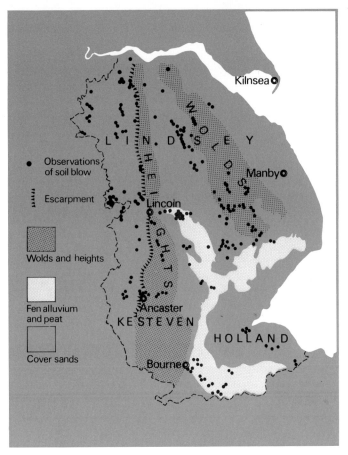

Fig 7.a

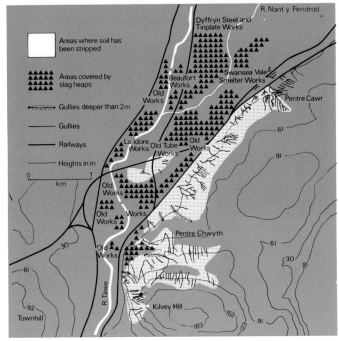

Areas where soil has been stripped

Areas covered by slag heaps

Gullies deeper than 2m

Gullies

Railways

Heights in m

Fig 7.b

of soil, subsoil and rock rubble removed in the last 100 to 150 years, assuming that an average depth of 65 cm has been transported downslope.

7.7 Comment on the following erosion factors:
(i) type and quantity of precipitation
(ii) type of bedrock
(iii) angle of slope
(iv) depth of soil.

7.8 Which areas are more vulnerable to erosion—those covered by bilberry or those covered by gorse and bracken? Why?

7.9 Suggest at least four measures you would take to stop this type of erosion.

Spreading deserts

7.10 Deserts are spreading all over the earth because of man's activities. Overgrazing on desert margins has resulted in soil degradation and erosion on a very large scale. Read the account from the *Guardian* (fig 7.c); and suggest, giving your reasons, which of the three eroded areas discussed above would benefit from applications of lignite and which would not.

7.11 Find an eroded area in your school grounds or in a recreation area, and calculate the volume of material removed and the probable rate of erosion. Try to study in detail an unaffected soil profile nearby for comparison.

7.12 In the field, find a wall running along the contour of a fairly steep slope of arable farmland, and compare the depth and nature of the soils on both sides of the wall.

Reclaiming deserts

The soils of desert margins are naturally more alkaline than most other soils, being particularly rich in chlorides and sulphates of magnesium, as well as those of sodium and calcium. Irrigation, if carelessly operated, increases the saline and alkaline content of these soils and renders them sterile. The irrigation water raises the water table, and the extra underground water eventually rises to the surface by capillarity as a result of evapotranspiration. The capillary water contains soluble salts in solution, which are deposited in the surface layers of the soil, so raising their salt content and rendering them unfit for plant growth.

exercises

7.13 Write an essay on the soils of hot deserts, referring to inputs from plants, animals and rocks, and to the limitations on soil formation and development.

Fig 7.c

Lignite used to halt advance of desert

By Anthony Tucker,
Science Correspondent

Trials in the Nile delta suggest that lignite—an abundant form of soft coal—may have the unexpected power to reverse the spread of deserts in some of the semi-arid areas of the earth.

Yields calculated to be at least three times those obtainable by normal husbandry on the delta sand have been achieved by introducing an additional 0.01 per cent of lignite into the top few millimetres of soil.

This finding may be important to the future pattern of agriculture and land reclamation in the vast semi-arid zones which is the subject of a major United Nations environmental programme conference, which opened at Nairobi yesterday.

The research in Britain revealed that lignite—in the right situations—provides the trace elements and organic constituents needed for the proper development of soil bacteria and root growth. As it works in to the soil it preogressively creates the conditions which permit the plant to take up nutrients.

One of the basic reasons for the loss of fertility in the arid zones is the breakdown of soil structure through the exhaustion of organic materials or the direct erosion of top soils. In areas where soil temperatures are high organic material is, in any case, broken down and lost very rapidly. One possible key to the apparent success of lignite is that it is only slowly soluble and is therefore retained as a source of organic nutrients for a long time.
(*Guardian* 30.5.77)

7.21

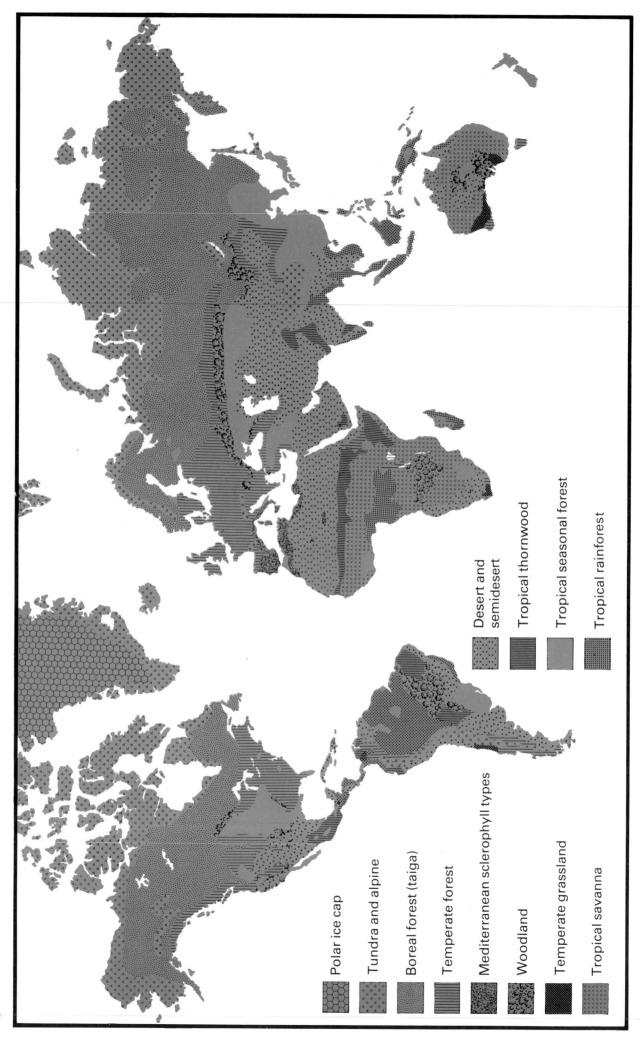

Fig 8.a

Polar ice cap
Tundra and alpine
Boreal forest (taiga)
Temperate forest
Mediterranean sclerophyll types
Woodland
Temperate grassland
Tropical savanna

Desert and semidesert
Tropical thornwood
Tropical seasonal forest
Tropical rainforest

8 World patterns

Net primary productivity: the creation of living matter

The most important characteristic of the earth's ecosystem is its productivity: the rate of creation of living matter by photosynthesis. On this rate depend all living things in the system—the plants, the animals and man.

Primary productivity is the RATE at which energy is bound or at which organic matter is created by photosynthesis, and is expressed as units of dry weight per unit area of the earth's surface per unit time. Primary productivity may be subdivided into gross and net productivities: GROSS primary productivity is the rate in dry grammes per square metre per year at which matter builds up in green plants before they respire; NET primary productivity is the gross rate reduced by the loss by respiration. Net production is available for man and other animals to harvest.

Fig 8.a shows the earth's major vegetation zones.

8.1 Using this map as a basis, together with the figures in table 8.b, shade in productivity zones of the earth's continents on another world map.

Zone	Net primary productivity (dry gm/m²/yr)
1	0 to 249
2	250 to 999
3	1 000 to 1 999
4	2 000 to 3 000

Comment on your findings.

Variation in primary productivity over the earth's surface is due primarily to variation in MOISTURE and TEMPERATURE; and secondarily to the different availabilities of NUTRIENTS and to the seral stage of PLANT SUCCESSION.

CARBON DIOXIDE and SUNLIGHT are less significant factors. Carbon dioxide is normally available everywhere in the atmosphere at concentrations of about 0.03% by volume. Sunlight varies in spectrum, intensity and duration with latitude, altitude, climate and pollution; but has less effect on plant growth than do the first four influences listed above. Its main effect is on the length of the growing season.

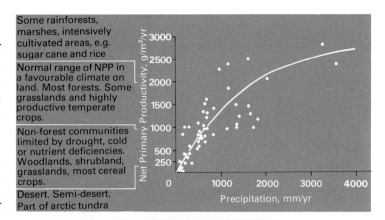

Some rainforests, marshes, intensively cultivated areas, e.g. sugar cane and rice

Normal range of NPP in a favourable climate on land. Most forests. Some grasslands and highly productive temperate crops.

Non-forest communities limited by drought, cold or nutrient deficiencies. Woodlands, shrubland, grasslands, most cereal crops.

Desert. Semi-desert. Part of arctic tundra

Fig 8.c

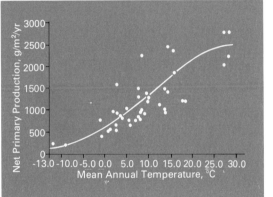

Fig 8.d

Table 8.b
Net primary productivity in different environments

	dry gm/ m²/yr
Tropical rainforest	2 2000
Tropical seasonal forest	1 600
Temperate forest	1 250
Boreal forest	800
Woodland and shrubland	700
Savanna	900
Temperate grassland	600
Tundra and alpine	140
Desert and semi-desert scrub	90
Extreme desert, rock sand and ice	3
Swamp and marsh	2 000
Lake and stream	250
Cultivated land	650
Average continental	773
Open ocean	125
Upwelling zones	500
Continental shelf	360
Alagal beds and reefs	2 500
Estuaries	1 500
Average marine	152
Average for whole earth	333

Water
Average water inputs over the earth's surface from precipitation are shown on world rainfall maps in your atlas. Plants need large amounts of water for transpiration, 700 to 1000 grammes on average being lost to the atmosphere for every gramme of biomass produced.

exercises

8.2 Look at fig 8.c and describe the relationship between net primary productivity and precipitation, commenting on the effects for very dry and very wet areas.

8.3 Precipitation in hot climates is less effective for primary productivity than in cool climates because of greater rates of evaporation. What other variable in precipitation could affect its usefulness to plant growth?

8.4 We are now able to comment on the net primary productivity of the places studied on pp. 4–13. Using an atlas world precipitation map, table 8.b and fig 8.c, estimate the rainfall and net primary productivity of the areas shown in figs 1.a–m. On your copy of fig 8.c, mark twelve points where you think the sites could lie. Account for any points that lie well away from the curve.

Temperature

8.5 Look at an atlas map of world annual temperatures and make a general statement about the relationship of temperature and latitude.

8.6 Look at fig 8.d. Estimate, for the middle part of the curve, the rough proportion by which productivity is increased for each 10° C.

Sunlight

8.7 Using table 8.e, draw a set of twelve parallel horizontal lines to compare the length of day each month in Britain, and a further set for day lengths at the equator.

8.8 Using table 8.f, draw two bar charts of the maximum possible monthly inputs of solar energy on a horizontal surface at 0° and 50°N. Why do the June inputs for 50°N exceed those at 0°?

8.9 Look at the figures in table 8.f and try to explain why maximum solar inputs anywhere on earth occur at 35°N and 40°N in June?

The two major influences, then, on net primary productivity on land are precipitation and temperature. The pattern of vegetation zones on the earth's surface can be largely explained in terms of precipitation and temperature.

Table 8e
Length of day at 51.7°N
(to nearest 5 mins)

	Hrs	mins
Jan.	8	40
Feb.	10	15
Mar.	12	00
April	14	20
May	15	55
June	16	40
July	15	55
Aug.	14	20
Sept.	12	00
Oct.	10	15
Nov.	8	40
Dec.	7	50

Nutrients

On land, nutrients available to plants are stored mainly in the soil. The variability in soil quality over the earth's surface is shown in fig 8.g.

exercises

8.10 Suggest the types of soil you would expect to find in the areas shown in figs 1.a–m. The major limitation on primary productivity in the oceans is that of nutrient supply. Loss of nutrients by sinking is greatest in the deepest oceans. The most productive parts of the oceans are on their fringes or where upwelling waters bring nutrients to the surface.

8.11 On a world map shade in areas of net primary productivity for the oceans (table 8.b). Use an atlas to delimit the three zones: open ocean, upwelling zones and continental shelf. Account for your distribution and comment on the following quotation[1]: 'The oceans are great and, taken as wholes, greatly productive, but the idea that they offer abundances of food awaiting harvest to feed hungry nations is an illusion'.

8.12 (i) Compare the total figures of net primary productivity for continents and oceans.
(ii) Compare the figure for temperate rainforest with that for open oceans.
Now write a page to describe and explain your findings, starting 'Although 70% of the earth's surface is covered with ocean . . .'

8.13 Describe and account for the distribution of three areas of low net primary productivity on the earth's surface.

8.14 Why do you think savanna lands have a higher net primary productivity than boreal forests?

8.15 Account for the high net primary productivity of tropical rainforest.

[1]R. H. Whittaker, *Communities and Ecosystems*, Macmillan, 2nd ed 1975, p. 213

Table 8.f Monthly inputs (maximum possible) of solar energy on horizontal surfaces at various latitudes north of the equator.
For southern latitudes, substitute the dates as follows.

N	June	May July	April August	Mar. Sept.	Feb. Oct.	Jan. Nov.	Dec.	S	Dec.	Nov. Jan.	Oct. Feb.	Sept. Mar.	Aug. April	July May	June

Kilocalories (1000 calories) per sq cm

Latitude N	J	F	M	A	M	J	Jy	A	S	O	N	D	Total
0°	18.5	17.6	19.8	18.6	18.2	17.3	18.2	19.2	19.2	19.5	17.9	17.9	221.9
5°	16.9	17.0	19.5	19.2	19.2	18.2	19.2	19.8	18.8	18.8	16.4	16.3	219.3
10°	16.0	16.2	19.5	19.5	20.1	19.2	20.1	20.1	18.8	17.9	15.5	15.0	217.9
15°	14.7	15.0	18.8	19.5	20.8	20.1	20.8	20.1	18.2	16.6	14.2	13.7	212.5
20°	13.1	14.1	18.5	19.8	21.4	20.7	21.4	20.4	17.9	15.6	12.7	12.1	207.7
25°	11.5	13.2	17.6	19.8	21.7	21.0	21.7	20.4	17.0	14.7	11.1	10.5	200.2
30°	10.2	11.8	16.3	19.5	21.7	21.3	21.7	20.1	15.8	13.1	9.9	8.9	190.3
35°	8.3	10.4	15.3	18.8	21.7	21.9	21.7	19.5	14.8	11.5	8.0	7.3	179.2
40°	7.0	9.2	14.4	17.9	21.4	21.9	21.4	18.5	13.9	10.2	6.8	5.7	168.3
45°	5.1	7.8	13.1	17.0	21.1	21.6	21.1	17.6	12.7	8.6	4.9	3.8	154.4
50°	3.5	6.3	11.5	16.4	20.4	21.3	20.4	16.9	11.1	7.0	3.4	2.9	141.1
55°	2.2	4.9	9.9	15.1	20.1	21.0	20.1	15.6	9.6	5.4	2.2	1.6	127.7

Fig 8.g

TUNDRA

L	organic layer
A1	light olive-brown acid silt loam
A2	blue-grey silt loam with yellow streaks
C	very dark-grey silt loam often permanently frozen
	permanently frozen layer preventing downward drainage

Solifluction and cryoturbation

Tundra soils are waterlogged in summer when frost in the surface layers melts to a depth ranging from two centimetres to several metres. The water cannot drain through the impermeable frozen layer beneath. The unfrozen layer may flow down a slope under gravity: SOLIFLUCTION. In the autumn the soil refreezes from the surface downwards. An unfrozen, waterlogged layer is trapped between the frozen surface and the permafrost and is subject to pressure and churning: CRYOTURBATION.

CHERNOZEM

A	horizons 100 cm deep
A	Deep layers of black loam. Good crumb structure. Rich in fauna
	Concentrations of calcareous material in lower horizons
C	Loess or loam

Formation

Chernozems develop under temperate grassland communities which produce large quantities of litter each year and where the soils are penetrated by many roots. Summer drought causes upward movement of water carrying salts in solution, deposited in the lower A horizons. Precipitation is low, minimizing leaching of nutrients. Winter frosts also inhibit nutrient breakdown and removal. So these soils are the richest in the world.

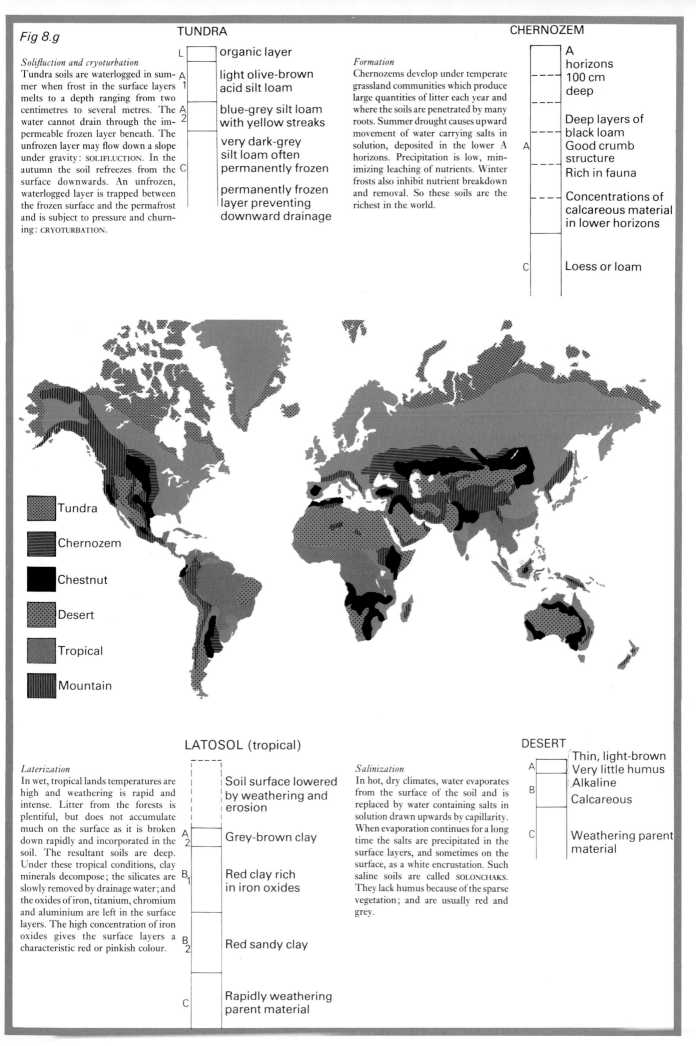

Tundra

Chernozem

Chestnut

Desert

Tropical

Mountain

LATOSOL (tropical)

	Soil surface lowered by weathering and erosion
A2	Grey-brown clay
B1	Red clay rich in iron oxides
B2	Red sandy clay
C	Rapidly weathering parent material

Laterization

In wet, tropical lands temperatures are high and weathering is rapid and intense. Litter from the forests is plentiful, but does not accumulate much on the surface as it is broken down rapidly and incorporated in the soil. The resultant soils are deep. Under these tropical conditions, clay minerals decompose; the silicates are slowly removed by drainage water; and the oxides of iron, titanium, chromium and aluminium are left in the surface layers. The high concentration of iron oxides gives the surface layers a characteristic red or pinkish colour.

DESERT

A	Thin, light-brown. Very little humus
B	Alkaline. Calcareous
C	Weathering parent material

Salinization

In hot, dry climates, water evaporates from the surface of the soil and is replaced by water containing salts in solution drawn upwards by capillarity. When evaporation continues for a long time the salts are precipitated in the surface layers, and sometimes on the surface, as a white encrustation. Such saline soils are called SOLONCHAKS. They lack humus because of the sparse vegetation; and are usually red and grey.

Biomass: the earth's resource

Biomass is the amount of organic matter present at a given time, per unit area of the earth's surface (dry gm/m² or dry tonnes/km²). It represents the accumulation over time, in plant and animal tissue, of chemical energy trapped by photosynthesis. Within obvious natural limits, biomass increases with the age of living things. The life-span of plants in general increases from deserts through shrublands and woodlands to forests; grasslands are excepted because they are annual. Biomasses of mature plant communities range as follows.

Table 8.h

	kg/m²
mature forests	20 to 60
woodlands	4 to 20
shrublands	2 to 10
grasslands	0.5 to 3
deserts and tundras	0 to 2

This accumulation of biomass over the earth's surface is an enormous resource which, until recently, man has irresponsibly plundered.

exercises

Look at table 8.j. The area of the earth's surface occupied by different vegetation zones is given in column 2, and the calculated value of total biomass present on the earth for the various plant communities is given in column 3. This indicates the distribution of resources over the earth's surface.

8.16 Calculate the contribution of all the earth's forests to the total world biomass and comment on your result.

8.17 Compare the contribution of forests to the earth's biomass with the biomass of the total marine area. The main reason for the difference is the relative stability of the two types of surface. Write a paragraph comparing plankton and forest trees in terms of nutrients available to them and biomass accumulated.

8.18 Why do you think the biomass in savannas is so low?

Table 8.j   Biomass on the earth's surface

	Biomass per unit area kg/m²	Area 10⁶ km²	Biomass 10⁹ t	Animal production 10⁶/t/yr	Animal biomass 10⁶ t
Tropical rain-forest	45	17.0	765	260	330
Tropical seasonal forest	35	7.5	260	72	90
Temperate forest	32	12.0	385	34	160
Boreal forest	20	12.0	240	38	57
Woodland and shrubland	6	8.5	50	30	40
Savanna	4	15.0	60	300	220
Temperate grassland	1.6	9.0	14	80	60
Tundra and alpine	0.6	8.0	5	3	3.5
Desert and semi-desert scrub	0.7	18.0	13	7	8
Extreme desert, rock, sand and ice	0.02	24.0	0.5	0.02	0.02
Swamp and marsh	15	2.0	30.0	32	20
Lake and stream	0.02	2.0	0.05	10	10
Cultivated land	1	14.0	14.0	9	6
TOTAL CONTINENTAL	12.3	149.0	1837	909	1005
Open ocean	0.003	332.0	1.0	2500	800
Upwelling zones	0.02	0.4	0.008	11	4
Continental shelf	0.01	26.6	0.27	430	160
Algal beds and reefs	2	0.6	1.2	36	12
Estuaries	1	1.4	1.4	48	21
TOTAL MARINE	0.01	361	3.9	3025	997
FULL TOTAL	3.6	510	1841	3934	2002

Biomass and plant succession

As we saw on pp. 14–24, the quantity of biomass present anywhere on earth is partly determined by the stage in plant succession: in the primary stage biomass is minimal, and in the climax stage it is at a maximum. During plant succession the biomass of the community increases because the rate of production of organic matter exceeds that of decomposition. The climatic climax community is in a steady state as the rates of photosynthesis and respiration, and of production and decomposition, are in balance.

Animal biomass

Calculations of animal biomass are speculative. Animal secondary production is less than 1% of net primary production on land and between 5 and 6% in the sea.

Marine animal production is mainly in the form of micro-organisms such as copepods which feed on phytoplankton. On land, animal biomass is concentrated in small short-lived arthropods, such as spiders and insects with segmented bodies and appendages, and in soil animals, such as mites and springtails. In forests, earthworms form the most massive group. This concentration of animal biomass in such lowly creatures is because of their food supply: they are the REDUCERS.

Ninety per cent of net primary productivity on land is consumed by reducers, a term which includes those eating live tissue, those eating dead material—for example scavengers—and decomposers—bacteria and fungi of decay. Detritus food chains may be diverse. A simple example is: plant tissue (death)—earthworms (death)—bacteria of decay. A more complicated example is: plant tissue (death)—fungi—millipede (faeces)—fungus in faeces—springtail (feeds on fungus)—predatory mite—centipede (death)—bacteria of decay.

exercises

In 1881 Charles Darwin recognized the importance of the earthworm, and *Humus and the Earthworm*, (Faber, 1966), makes easy, enjoyable and informative reading.

8.19 Compare the total animal biomass on land with that in the sea. (See table 8.j, column 5.) Your answer may be surprising in view of the respective total plant biomasses available for consumption in the two areas. The reason may be that the tissue of most land plants is hard and so difficult for animals to eat, whereas phytoplankton is easily consumed by zooplankton.

8.20 Why do you think animal biomass in savanna areas is relatively high?

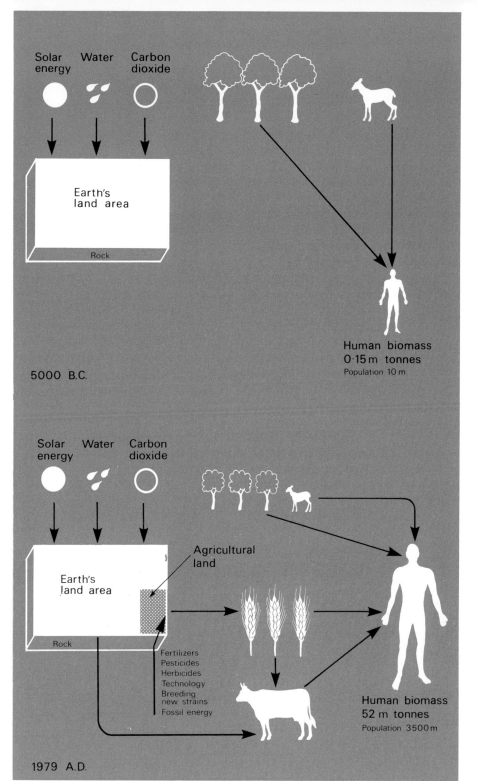

Fig 8.k

The influence of man on biomass

The earth's human biomass is about 52 million tonnes—slightly less than that of all the earthworms! The growth of human population (see fig 8.k) is the result of man's using his intelligence and enterprise to develop the earth's resources; though he has reduced the variety of plant and animal species. The increase in available resources has caused a reduction in human death rates and a further increase in human population. This is not the normal pattern of population dynamics and ecological regulation that we saw on pp. 4–13. The rest of the earth has suffered: the explosion in human population has resulted in environmental degradation, in shortage of food and other resources, and in adverse psychological effects in man. These effects could, of course, eventually restore the balance of nature! We need to understand better the functioning of the earth's ecosystem, to curb our greed and to arrive at a wiser policy of long-term management of planet earth.

Husbanding resources

Man is beginning to realise that some resources on earth may soon be exhausted and cannot be replaced. Table 8.1 lists resources according to their renewability. As man's numbers increase and resources dwindle, there is an urgent need to evaluate all the various possibilities for land and to plan land development very carefully.

Table 8.1

Inexhaustible resources	Exhaustible but renewable resources	Exhaustible and irreplaceable resources
Total amounts of: Atmosphere Water Rock Solar energy	Water in usable condition Vegetation Animal life Human populations Certain soil minerals Uncontaminated CO_2 and O_2 where needed Certain ecosystem types	Soil Certain minerals Rare species Certain ecosystem types Landscape in natural condition Much of the groundwater supply

exercises

LAND-USE PLANNING: EVALUATING LAND FOR AGRICULTURAL PURPOSES

8.21 We can make observations and tests in the field in order to grade agricultural land: possible crops, the level and consistency of yield and the cost of obtaining the crop. Long-term limitations which affect farming are mainly physical: climate, soil and slope. These three factors in turn need detailed examination (see fig 8.m). In assessing land for farming, such factors as stoniness and slope are significant because they may affect the use of farm machinery.

You should evaluate an area of approximately 20 × 20 m—the precise area is not critical. Find climatic data from soil memoirs, and record details of soil and slope in the field. Then summarize each of the three factors, climate, soil and slope, as being favourable, moderately unfavourable or severe. Finally combine these three descriptions to give a grade between I and V for the land as a whole.

Grades of land

Grade I has only minor limitations: soils are deep, rich, well-drained, water-retentive loams or peats on fairly level sites, with a climate allowing the easy cultivation of most crops.

Grade II has minor limitations such as texture, depth or drainage of the soil, or exposure or slope.

Grade III has moderate limitations which restrict the choice of crop, timing of cultivation, or crop yield. It includes land in western Britain where rainfall is over 1150 mm or with slopes 1 in 8 to 1 in 5. Grass and cereals are the main crops on this land.

Fig 8.m

```
                        LAND CAPABILITY WORKSHEET
                                                        Date _____

    SITE      Name _____
                                                        Grid Ref _____
              Approximate area _____ sq/m
                                                        Height above MSL _____
              Present land use _____

  I CLIMATE   Rainfall _____ mm/yr
              Temperatures _____ °C
              Evapo-transpiration _____ mm/yr
              Exposure (e.g. exposed to strong easterly
                        wind)_____     Summary of climate (F,U,S) _____

 II SOIL      Depth (>20,25,50,75cm) _____
              Stoniness (none,slight,stony,very stony,
                        extremely stony) _____
              Erosion hazard (F,U,S) _____
              Texture (sandy,loamy or clayey) _____
              Structure (platy,blocky,prismatic,
                        crumby) _____
              Water retention (gm/gm of soil) _____    Summary of soil (F,U,S) _____

III SLOPE     Gradient (>7°,12°,16°,25°) _____
              Drainage (good,imperfect,poor,
                        very poor) _____    Summary of slope (F,U,S) _____


                                                        SOIL GRADE _____
                                                           (I - V)

    F = Favourable   U = Moderately unfavourable  S = Severe
```

Answers to *exercises*

Grade IV has severe limitations. It includes land over 200 m with over 1300 mm of rain per year or land with slopes between 1 in 5 and 1 in 3. A high proportion is under grass.

Grade V has very severe limitations, for instance land over 330 m with more than 1500 mm rain per year or with slopes greater than 1 in 3. It is generally under grass or rough grazing.

Land-use planning on a world scale

8.22 Four categories of land may be recognized according to the standard of living and density of population:

(i) under-developed and relatively sparsely populated lands;

(ii) under-developed densely populated lands;

(iii) less densely populated lands with a high standard of living;

(iv) densely populated developed lands.

Choose an example of each of these four categories from figs 1.a–m, and produce plans for their future development, bearing in mind the following guidelines.

Classify the resources (living and abiotic) shown in the photographs into

(a) renewable and

(b) non-renewable.

Consider the following factors: the need for capital and technological information, cultural considerations, possible problems of labour supply and land shortage (in some cases need for land redevelopment).

In making decisions on land use, one ultimately needs to compromise between the claims of culture, economics, aesthetics and conservation. Man not only needs warmth, shelter and food but also peace and harmony. By trying to understand the functioning of ecosystems he may eventually satisfy all these needs without degrading or destroying the environment and consequently himself.

1.20 (ii) Shark. (iii) Eagle.

1.21 Oxygen, sulphur.

1.23 Uplift of submarine surface to form land.

1.24 Faster.

1.25 (i) It would stay the same.
(ii) Drop.

1.26 (i) Rose leaves decreased and ladybirds increased.
(ii) Greenfly decreased because of (i). State of balance returned.

2.44 Rain washes alkaline material down in soil. Acid litter added in zone 4.

4.4 339062.5 cu cm.

4.5 2712500 cu cm.

4.6 27125 cu cm.

4.7 40687.5 cu cm.

4.8 23191.875 dry gm/m²

4.9 579.79687 dry gm/m²/yr.

4.10 681.84112 dry gm/m²/yr.

4.14 67.67 kilocals/cm²/yr.

4.24 928 cu cm/m²/yr.

4.33 NUTRIENTS (in g/m²/yr)

Enter figures in the boxes in your sketch of fig 4.t.

	Nitrogen	Phosphorus	Potassium	Calcium	Magnesium	Sodium	Carbon
Litter fall	4.10	0.22	1.05	2.38	0.39	0.17	196.22
Leaching from plants	−0.07	0.09	2.51	0.99	0.47	2.02	17.52
INPUT Dust	0.96	0.04	0.30	0.73	0.46	3.53	5.26

INPUT Solar energy 6.767 cals/m²/yr

INPUT Rain 928 cu cm/m²/yr

Plants: primary producers 681.84 g/m²/yr

6.12 £132.57/ha.

6.13 £144 (farming company) − £132.57 (Forestry Commission) = £11.43.

6.21 160 dry gm/m²/yr.

6.23 dry gm/m²/yr.

6.24 160 dry gm/m²/yr.

7.4 (i) Between 1250 000 and 1875 000 tonnes.
(ii) Between 6250 and 9375 tonnes/yr.

7.6 130 000 000 000 cu cm.

Index

Abiotic substances 10
Ainsdale 20, 21
Animal biomass 60, 61
Animal productivity 50
Arctic alpine vegetation 26, 27, 29
Arresting factors 15, 16
Autotrophs 11

Biomass 12, 49, 60
Biomass calculation 32
Biosphere 10

Catena 46
Clarke, G. R. 46
Clements, Frederick 25
Chernozem 59
Climatic change 8
Climatic climax vegetation 16, 24, 25, 28, 60
Climatic data 26, 33, 58
Coleman, Alice 53
Colonization 14–17
Conservation 51, 53, 62, 63
Consumers 11
Cryoturbation 59

Darwin, Charles 61
Decomposers 11
Deserts 7, 8, 9, 25, 26, 27, 55, 56, 57, 60
Dokuchayev, Vasily 43

Earthworm 61
Ecological niche 11
Ecological regulation 12, 61
Ecosystem 10, 11, 12, 15, 34
Ecotone 34, 35
Equilibrium 11

Farming 5, 6, 8, 9, 49–51, 53, 54, 62, 63
Field capacity 44
Flaxmere 22, 23
Food chain 10, 11, 12, 20, 21
Food web 35, 36
Forestry 7, 50–51
Fylingdales Moor 51–53

Gleying 40

Habitat 4, 8, 10
Habitat classification 4, 11
Halosere 18–24

Hatchmere 22, 23
Heterotrophs 11
Human biomass 61
Human population 61
Hydrosere 23, 24

Incas 9

Jenny, H. 43

Keen of Hamar 25, 26, 27
Krakatoa 16, 17

Landscape classification 4
Land use 47–53, 62–63
Land-use planning 62–63
Laterization 59
Leaching 40
Lemmings 27
Limiting factors 11, 12, 13, 25
Lincolnshire 54
Lithosere 24
Lockton Low Moor 45–47, 48–49

Man's activities 4, 8, 27, 46, 49, 50, 51, 54, 61
Mapwork 25, 28, 44, 45, 47, 51, 53, 54, 62, 63
Marsh 18–19, 22, 23, 60
Mechanical eluviation 40
Milne, G. 46
Model 11
Montgomeryshire upland 54
Moorland 7, 17, 46, 47

Newgate Wood 32, 33, 45
Nutrient cycle 11, 12, 13, 34

Oak woodland 29, 34
Oceans 27, 57, 58–60

Parent material 38–43
Parkgate 18–19
Peat 39
Permafrost 27
Peruvian Indians 9
Photosynthesis 10, 11, 12
Plant community 27, 34
Plant growth 25
Plant succession 15, 16, 18, 19, 20–21, 57, 60
Podzolization 40
Population density 8

Population dynamics 4, 12–13, 61
Precipitation 33–57
Predation 10
Primary productivity 12, 32, 48, 50, 53, 57, 58–61
Producers 11
Psammosere 20–21, 24

Rabbits 36
Reducers 61
Rothamsted farming productivity 53

Saharan cave painting 8
Salinization 59
Sand dunes 20–21
Savannah 4, 56, 57, 58, 60, 61
Seral stage 16, 17, 18, 19, 20, 21, 23, 24, 57, 60
Slope 30, 43
Soils 17, 21, 23, 26, 37–46
Soil classification 42
Soil erosion 54–55
Soil formation 15, 16, 18–19, 20–21, 39–40
Soil processes 40, 41, 59
Soil profile 29, 30, 37, 40, 41, 45
Soil survey 29, 30, 42, 44
Soil texture 38–39
Soil water 43, 44
Solar energy 10, 12, 32, 58
Solifluction 59
Solonchak 59
Specific weights of woods 36
Stamp, Dudley 53
Stratification of vegetation 34
Subclimax 16, 20
Surtsey 14, 15
Swansea Valley 54

Technology 8
Temperature 58
Trophic level 11, 12
Tropical forest 6, 56, 57, 60
Tundra 5, 27, 56, 57, 59

Vegetation survey 17, 22, 23, 25, 29, 30, 32, 33, 34, 36

Vegetation zones 56, 57

Water 57
Woodlands 29–37, 56, 57, 60
World vegetation zones 57–60

Xerosere 24